BRITAIN IN OLD PHO

Forgotten Thames

BRIAN EADE

SUTTON PUBLISHING

Sutton Publishing Limited
Phoenix Mill · Thrupp · Stroud
Gloucestershire · GL5 2BU

First published 2002

Title page: 'Fishy' Jack at Benson lock, 1930s.

British Library Cataloguing in Publication Data
A catalogue record for this book is available from the British Library.

ISBN 0-7509-2818-2

Typeset in 10.5/13.5 Photina.
Typesetting and origination by
Sutton Publishing Limited.
Printed and bound in England by
J.H. Haynes & Co. Ltd, Sparkford.

For Uncle Jack

CONTENTS

No sign of the lock-keeper? Perhaps he's gone to 'Lyonch'. Invented by the publicity department at Lyons to encourage more people to patronize their teashops at lunchtime, the catchphrase 'Where's George?' was popular in the 1930s and endured until the outbreak of the Second World War. (*Author*)

INTRODUCTION

Philosophers tell us that we never see the same river twice. True enough; the Thames is constantly developing and evolving, sometimes of its own accord and sometimes aided by man. Either way, images from around 100 years ago amply demonstrate just how much change has been wrought upon England's most famous river.

Over the centuries many parties have been interested in controlling the flow of river: millers and monks who needed a good head of water to turn the wheels of their mills; professional fishermen who constructed elaborate eel traps and fish weirs; and lastly barge operators, who were frequently stranded on shoals owing to lack of water, kept waiting and then, to add insult to injury, compelled to pay a toll before they could pass through. With so many vested interests concerned with the Thames and no overall governing body, there was often conflict and frequent flooding.

The flow of the River Thames has been controlled in one form or another for centuries. In 1197, King Richard I commanded that 'all weirs that are in the Thames be removed'. Later, to fund crusades to the Holy Land, he sold his rights over the river to the City of London. A clause in Magna Carta, signed by King John at Runnymede in 1215, mentioned the removal of 'kiddles' from the river. (An ancient French term meaning 'a stake fence in a stream'. It is probably from this word we obtain the expression 'kettle of fish'.)

Until 1350 it fell to the royals to look after the river through a number of intermediaries or commissioners and in that year an Act of Parliament passed by Edward III prohibited obstruction of the navigable Thames. In 1605 James I appointed eighteen commissioners to sort out all the navigation problems between Oxford and Burcot, but by 1611 they had ceased to be effective. Twelve years passed and then a second Oxford–Burcot Commission became responsible for taxes, sewers and river purity, but most importantly, they had the power to install locks and weirs, which they did at Iffley, Sandford and Swift Ditch. An Act of 1751 introduced the Thames Navigation Commission. This organization controlled the Thames upstream from Staines but with a membership of 600 commissioners it proved to be unwieldy. However, this commission had powers to purchase land, weirs and towpaths for improvements and to some extent it was successful, building eight pound locks between 1771 and 1772 and all the locks between Oxford and Staines from 1815 onwards.

The Thames Conservancy was formed by Act of Parliament in 1857 and became the forerunner of the modern conservation movement, implementing vast changes and improved management of the Thames, dredging, building new locks and dismantling all the flash weirs that were the legacy of earlier times. Some of its most notable achievements include the digging of the Desborough Channel at Weybridge and the mechanization of most of the locks. This auspicious body served and conserved the River Thames until 1974.

The river scenery 100 years ago bore little or no resemblance to the ordered and efficiently managed river of today. Methods of controlling the flow of water evolved from simple dams across the river via numerous changes and modifications to today's modern weirs. Despite this progress, however, some weir structures dating back to Victorian times are still in use today. One of the earliest types was the 'flash' weir, so called because the vessel passed downstream on a 'flash' of released water. Going upstream was much more difficult, with the craft either being towed or winched against the flow. This type of weir developed from the wide variety of dams, weirs and obstructions placed across the river by millers, landowners or fishermen. These early structures were often named after the men who built or owned them – Skinner's, Ridge's and Hart's to name but three. All of these flash weirs have been dismantled to become locks or weir channels. The locations of some, such as Medley Weir above Oxford, are still recognizable from the riverbanks and weir cottages. The Thames Conservancy dismantled the last operating flash weir at Medley in 1937 as part of a scheme to alleviate flooding above Oxford.

Millers often owned both a mill and a flash weir or lock. Frequently the mill business was given priority over the flash weir, causing delays and conflict with barge operators. The so-called 'merrie' miller was more than happy to let you pass his mill (for a fee) but very often only at a time that suited him. Many of the mills that were built along the Thames served two purposes: deepening and stabilizing the river, and, of course, providing the power, via a waterwheel, for grinding corn. Most mills had wooden gears and it is thought that, as was often the case with windmills, fires caused by the friction between these wheels may have led to the demise of the mills at Iffley and Streatley. Mill usage varied greatly. In addition to grinding corn, they were also used for making cloth, cattle feed, thimbles and oil. In later years production moved to gunpowder, copper utensils and even brown paper. When trading ceased mills were sold on relatively cheaply, and more recently stylish and desirable waterfront properties have been built on these sites.

Up to the mid-nineteenth century, the Thames was a major trade route with a vast array of goods travelling in both directions. These goods were loaded on to barges at the numerous wharves along the river and then towed to their destinations by teams of horses. Where the towpath changed banks, often as a result of a landowner dispute, a ferry service had to be provided to take the horses across. At one time these ferries were more numerous than locks, with the towpath sometimes changing banks several times over a short distance. Keen Edge, Gatehampton and Spade Oak ferries have vanished along with the trade that sustained them, although in some cases the ferry houses are still in existence, albeit in private ownership.

More conspicuous and certainly more enduring river crossings are the familiar Thames bridges. Early versions were usually made of wood and, as such, often rotted fairly swiftly at the waterline. Replacements were built with differing degrees of success and in a variety of styles ranging from elegant to functional. Despite these changes many bridges that we see today remain virtually untouched apart from essential repairs; others, such as Walton Bridge, seem to be forever blighted with ugly and temporary status. Frequently, the construction of new bridges had to be paid for either by public subscription or by charging a toll for those wishing to cross.

With the possible exception of the Thames Traditional Boat Society, few hand-propelled craft venture out on the river now. Yet, in 1900 the opposite was true with large queues of skiffs and punts congregating at the more popular locks such as Boulters and Molesey. At that time river traffic was changing in nature from commercial to pleasure and the Victorians embraced this aspect of life wholeheartedly. Sumptuous, elegant and ornate houseboats once graced the Thames at every turn, often travelling to Henley each year for the regatta, and there was even a houseboat that served teas! The few that have survived are now confined to small, well-organized, residential moorings.

London once boasted the largest dock system in the world, with goods arriving from and departing to all corners of the globe. It richly deserved the informal title 'Warehouse of the World'. Most of the major docks are still there, although one of the first, the East India at Blackwall, now has only a basin to remind us of its existence. On the south side of the river, the majority of the enormous Surrey docks have gone completely, leaving only Greenland, South, Surrey basin and part of Canada Water. It was largely because of the docks that the oldest police service in the world, the Thames Police, was formed in 1798 at Wapping to prevent the wholesale theft of cargo. It was estimated that over a third of personnel working in or around the docks at that time were known thieves or receivers of stolen goods. Patrolling from Staines in the west down to Dartford in the estuary, they provide a useful addition to the land-based patrols.

In only 100 years or so the River Thames has altered in many significant ways. One could argue that the river has lost some of its charm, but riparian owners are pleased that their properties are no longer at risk from flooding. Whatever your viewpoint, the next 100 years will certainly bring about further changes, but they are unlikely to be as significant those that took place during the last century.

1

Seven Springs to Swift Ditch Lock

Rivers rise from more than one source and the Thames is no exception. Despite years of argument and debate by academics and historians about where the Thames begins, there remains an element of doubt. Seven Springs may well be the 'real source' of the Thames, rising much higher than Thames Head, near Cricklade, the official source.

The section of the river between Seven Springs and Swift Ditch lock has arguably seen the most changes in the last 100 years and the quaintly named weirs, bridges and flash locks that caused so many navigation problems in the past have all been swept away, not by the river, but by the authorities. This was a protracted process and the last few to succumb were Eaton Hastings, Eynsham, Kings and Medley, all above Oxford.

Anyone who has navigated the river at Folly Bridge, Oxford, will soon discover why the forgotten lock and weir were removed and the navigation channel altered in favour of a more direct route. Evidence of the old lock still remains visible, should you take the older route by accident, although the lock cottage has been demolished to make way for student accommodation.

After 350 years of neglect the historic Swift Ditch lock near Abingdon, one of the first Thames pound locks, has recently undergone a full structural and archaeological survey and some remedial work to prevent further decay. Full restoration to its former glory awaits this lock, and one can only hope the will and the finances become available. There is now an information board at Swift Ditch, finally acknowledging the site's historical significance.

The caption on this 1930s postcard reads: 'Seven Springs, source of the River Thames'. It is possible that these springs were once considered to be the source as they rise higher than the official origin of the river at Thames Head. They are, of course, the source of the River Churn, a major tributary of the Thames. There are two stones here bearing the same Latin inscription: 'Hic tuus o tamesine pater septemgeminus fons', loosely translated as 'Here are your seven sources/founts, o father Thames'. Draw your own conclusions. (*Mary Clarke*)

Cricklade has long been associated with the upper limit of navigation of the river, although it is doubtful few boats would pass along this channel, photographed in about 1865. It was close to this rickety bridge, known locally as Plank Bridge, that the last full immersion baptism in the Thames took place twelve years later. (*The Environment Agency and The River & Rowing Museum*)

Inside the derelict Inglesham lock on the Thames and Severn canal looking towards its junction with the River Thames, 1950s. Proposals to join the Thames with the River Severn were discussed as long ago as 1634, eventually bearing fruit in 1789. (*Chris Groves*)

A distant view of Kempsford church, photographed by Henry Taunt *c*. 1900. As the name suggests, there was an important ford established here when the River Thames formed the boundary between the two feudal kingdoms of Wessex and Mercia. (*The Environment Agency*)

The town of Lechlade once profited from the excavation of the Thames and Severn canal, which was opened to traffic in 1789. From Lechlade wharf, seen here, a wide variety of goods were carried down to London including 'great weights of cheese'. Goods travelling from Gloucester and the River Severn made their way here, although there was little in the way of return trade. As with many canals, trade declined in the face of competition from the railways and the canal closed in 1927. (*Mary Clarke*)

In the winter of 1962/3 the Thames was frozen for a long time at Halfpenny Bridge, Lechlade, and in many other places. Perhaps a strong faith led these two to believe that the ice would not crack under their combined weight. The picture was taken by a local press photographer. (*David Wilson & Lynn David*)

Looking downstream to St John's lock with the old lock-cottage situated on an island. This photograph was certainly taken before 1905 when this cottage was demolished. A new property was later built on the opposite bank in a style similar to the weir cottage at Medley, near Oxford. (*Ken Townsend*)

Eaton Hastings weir, 1883. This is sometimes referred to as Hart's weir. It had the advantage of having the Anchor Inn nearby and ready to provide refreshment for those who had hauled boats through the flash weir. Often innkeepers looked after this type of weir, no doubt benefiting from both tolls and beer sales. The Thames Conservancy removed the weir in 1937 as part of their Upper Thames Improvements and the Anchor Inn was destroyed by fire in 1979, with the tragic loss of three lives. (*Oxfordshire County Council Photographic Archive*)

Harper's Bridge, *c.* 1890, probably named after the owner or keeper of Harper's weir, which may have also been the alternate name for Radcot lock. The occupants of these cottages were said to 'till the earth and fish the water' in their endeavours to eke out a living. This bridge was most likely taken down in 1894. (*The Environment Agency and The River & Rowing Museum*)

Ridges weir was often called 'Rudges' weir and all that remains of it is a footbridge marked on modern maps as Hart's footbridge. Perhaps it was given this name because the ever-present Hart family operated a ferry nearby. In 1866, the toll for a boat was 4*d* and a canal boat had to pay 1*s* to pass through. The weir was probably taken down in about 1879 because it was noted as 'now removed' in 1880. (*The Environment Agency and The River & Rowing Museum*)

12th Berks.(U.T.P.) Bn. Home Guard.
(A.1. Coy.)

2nd May, 1944

Dear Lt. Carter,

I have been trying to get you on the phone since yesterday, but your phone is out of order and had not been reported, so I have reported the matter for you as it is most essential that telephonic communication with you is maintained at the present time.

The matter I wanted to speak to you about concerns the guard by members of your Platoon on Sunday night. Firstly a new 1 lb. packet of sugar was put out on Sunday for use containing 114 lumps and a notice on the packet stating that only 16 lumps are to be used by each nightly guard. The following morning it was reported that only about ¼ lb. remained, and I went along myself and counted the lumps and only 31 remained, which means that your men took 83 lumps on Sunday night.

This is a serious matter as we are only allowed 1 lb. of sugar and ½ lb. of tea per week to provide two hot drinks to the guard during the night. In consequence the other 6 guards this week have only 31 pieces between them (5 per night) whereas your men used 83 pieces on one night. You will please take this matter up with your men as soon as possible and instruct your Guard Commander to see that this does not occur again. The Guard last night also reported that the mantle of one Tilley lamp was broken.

Yours sincerely

[signature]
Catt A⅃

Lt. Carter,
Shifford Manor Farm,
Nr. Witney.

The 'Sugar Cubes Affair'. It would be easy to dismiss this letter as a product of the mind of an over-zealous officer. However, there was a serious side to the contents, with regular patrols established along the Thames during the Second World War to counter the very real threat of enemy invasion. There were other defences along the river including pillboxes, gun emplacements, tank traps and ditches. Most have survived and a profusion of pillboxes can be seen by the river near Buscot. (*Nigel Dawe*)

As outlined earlier, many modern locks started their lives as weirs, including this one at Rushey, seen here *c.* 1890. It made sense to build a pound lock at a site where there was already some form of water control. Some years ago the lock-keeper was asked, 'What hours do you work?' by an elderly lady. He replied '9 a.m. until sunset, madam'. She then enquired, 'How do you know when it is sunset if it is cloudy?' (*The Environment Agency and The River & Rowing Museum*)

Bablock Hythe ferry, *c.* 1900. In Anglo-Saxon English, the word 'hythe' means wharf or stage. Whether there was either here remains a matter of conjecture. A ferry has been operating here for over 700 years and you can still cross to the pub in the summer if the landlord is operating a ferry that day. (*British Waterways Board*)

Skinner's weir, 1888. Studying images of these ancient and somewhat dilapidated structures serves as a reminder of the difficulties encountered navigating the river above Oxford, where each owner of a weir charged a toll to pass. The weir, the Fish Inn and later bridge have all gone from this site, leaving hardly any trace of their existence. (*The Environment Agency and The River & Rowing Museum*)

Lock-keeper Albert Wright struggling to steer an unruly barge up to Northmoor lock in preparation for his move down to Pinkhill lock in the late 1950s. His reason for moving? Pinkhill had electricity! (*Chris Groves*)

Pinkhill lock, *c*. 1865. It was at this tranquil place that one lock-keeper teased a local fisherman about how easy it was to make a catch. Knowing that a large chub often lurked in the lock, the keeper bet the angler that he could catch something within five minutes and not only that, he would name the fish – a chub. Fetching his rod and bait, the keeper pretended to fish intently for a couple of minutes and then cast to where he knew the chub would be waiting. The fish took the bait instantly and the keeper landed the fish. The angler couldn't believe his eyes. 'Too easy', the keeper said and pocketed the bet. (*The Environment Agency and The River & Rowing Museum*)

Lock-keeper Albert Wright makes his way across the flooded meadows at Pinkhill in the late 1950s. For many lock-keepers, the only way into or out of their remote lock-houses was by boat. Upstream at Northmoor, even after an access road was built, the farmer insisted on field gates, making it necessary to leave the vehicle sixteen times before reaching the lock-house. (*Chris Groves*)

Numerous weirs have been built in the vicinity of Eynsham and this one may have been referred to as 'Boldes' or 'Swithen's'. Most likely built by local monks for catching fish, there has been a weir in existence here since about 1539. This image, probably dating from 1900, shows the crude nature of early weirs. (*Oxfordshire County Council Photographic Archive*)

The Thames Conservancy launch *Ember* making its way upstream on a flash through Eynsham flash lock with the *Loddon* and *Coln* following in the distance. There were strict rules governing these flashes and even a timetable for them. Eynsham's flash could take place on Mondays at 5 p.m. and Thursdays at 8 p.m. These locks were built to a wide variety of designs. Here, one half of the dam across the river consists of paddles and rymers, while the other is a single beam gate operated by pushing the beam. (*The Environment Agency*)

TELEGRAPHIC ADDRESS:
"CONSERVANCY, ESTRAND, LONDON"
TELEPHONES:
LOCAL-GERRARD 5855
TRUNK-GERRARD 5856

Memorandum

From the Secretary,
Thames Conservancy.

2 & 3, Norfolk Street,
Strand, W. C. 2.

T.S.

To   23rd November, 1926.

the Lock-keepers,
Weirkeepers and Ferrymen.

Complaints have been received from firms trading upon the River that a serious leakage occurs during transit between the point of loading and the point of discharge of commodities such as coal, timber, etc., and all Lock-keepers are directed to assist, as far as they are able, to detect any interference with cargoes while vessels are in the vicinity of their locks, and to report any cases of pilfering or unauthorised removal of any goods from barges.

Lock-keepers, Weir-keepers and Ferrymen are particularly warned against receiving or purchasing from persons in charge of craft, any merchandise whatsoever, and any case of a Conservators' employee so doing, will be severely dealt with.

Please insert this order in your Book of Instructions.

Goods being transported by barge frequently went missing and lock-keepers were cautioned against involvement in such disappearances by this quaintly worded letter. At one lock the keeper helped himself to a lump of coal each time a coal barge came through. By the arrival of winter he had enough fuel for the lock-house, as well as the lock office stove. (*Bill McCreadie*)

King's weir. *c.* 1890. It is thought that a weir has been in existence here for over 450 years. There was often conflict with the owners of the nearby Wolvercote Mill. On one occasion in 1813 this resulted in some stone throwing at lock-keeper Hart for not maintaining sufficient water. This weir remained a flash pass with boat rollers until 1927 when a new lock and house were built, cutting the corner of the river. (*The Environment Agency and The River & Rowing Museum*)

Scribbled on the reverse of this photograph are the words '*Consuta* running at 20 miles per hour'. The vessel was built in 1895 by the Saunders Patent Launch Building Syndicate of Goring, and Consuta was also the name given to this type of construction, which was patented by Sam Saunders. Shortly after the invention of laminated and glued hulls, Sam decided that 'sewing' the hull together with annealed copper wire would make a more durable craft. This super-light and fast boat was used by the BBC to film the Varsity Boat Races until 1955. (*The Warborough and Shillingford History Society*)

The former Godstow cut was so infested by weeds when it was photographed in 1880 that boats had to be towed along. When the original channel was dug in 1770, the navvies unearthed some coffins, prompting an outcry. In 1885 the Thames Conservancy widened the channel and once again several stone coffins from the nunnery were disturbed. Small boys were seen playing with the excavated skulls and bones, and although the coffins were reburied near the east wall of the nunnery, many tombs had been severely disturbed. One coffin had two skulls inserted and others had the wrong bones replaced; another even included animal bones. Of the ten coffins found at that time, none had their lids, but two had unusual crosses on them and dated from the early thirteenth century. The boat in the channel holds a shooting party, one of whom seems to be pointing a gun towards the photographer! On the left are the ruins of the 'house of nonnes' and in the distance the popular riverside pub, the Trout Inn. (*The Bodleian Library, University of Oxford, Ms Top Oxon d502 fol82*)

Probably photographed at the beginning of the twentieth century, The Perch pub at Binsey has considerably altered from the time when H. Edmonds sold Higgins's ales. Nearby is a pool named Black Jack's Hole, where it was proposed in 1787 to build a lock. Instead the decision went in favour of building the lock at Godstow. (*The Environment Agency and The River & Rowing Museum*)

Walking the greasy pole at Port Meadow, *c.* 1900. This was probably a University event judging by the stern of a college barge visible to the right of the photograph. This meadow has been Oxford's perpetual saviour from serious flooding, and despite attempts to build upon it, it remains largely unaltered. However, during the First World War, there was an airfield here with temporary hangars and the silhouettes of aircraft laid out in stones for target practice. The seeds of many new species of flora arrived here on the undercarriages of aircraft. (*Oxfordshire County Council Photographic Archive*)

At Medley, the Thames has many channels and this weir spans the old navigation route leading to Castle Mills. On a warm summer evening in 1870 hundreds of freshwater crayfish could be seen below this weir but unfortunately disease has now wiped them out, although they are still to be found in the River Kennet. Medley had the distinction of being the last operational flash weir on the River Thames, but it was dismantled in 1937 and only the weir cottage remains. (*Steve Capel-Davies*)

In December 1885 the decayed centre arch of the old stone bridge at Osney collapsed, sweeping away with it a man and two girls. The man and one girl survived but, sadly, eleven-year-old Rhoda Miles drowned and her body was not discovered until three years later. The replacement bridge, seen here under construction in 1888, cost around £1,200 and with a span over 50 ft and low headroom, it effectively cut off the Upper Thames to larger boats. (*Oxfordshire County Council Photographic Archive*)

Osney Mill, photographed *c.* 1890, was probably built in about 1129, shortly after the foundation of the nearby abbey. For over 800 years this mill ground corn and bones. It then raised nap on cloth and later became a sawmill. It even produced gunpowder during the Civil War. It was rebuilt about 1845, but finally stopped work in 1965. The lock that shows much evidence of decay and neglect has fared better than the mill and has been considerably improved. (*The Bodleian Library, University of Oxford, Ms Minn 228 fol60*)

Looking downstream to Folly weir in 1887, with Oxford's waterworks on the left. The main navigation channel used to pass to the right of the island, but at such an awkward angle that barges often became stuck in the arch of the bridge. Folly Bridge acquired its name in about 1650 because of the folly built upon it. It had previously been known as 'Graundpont' (large bridge) and had a causeway of at least forty arches heading south over the marshes towards Abingdon. (*The Bodleian Library, University of Oxford, Ms Top Oxon d493*)

A rare photograph taken in 1860 of the short-lived Folly lock at Folly Bridge. Built in about 1793, it had only the one set of gates (visible in this photograph) and a fall of about 3 ft. The gates were removed in 1884, establishing a free passage through. The tiny wooden lock-house relating to this lock has recently been demolished. To the right of the lock are the premises of J. Salter, boat-builders, established in 1858, now steamer operators. (*The Bodleian Library, University of Oxford, Ms Top Oxon d493 fol29*)

Looking downstream from Folly Bridge, this photograph was probably taken during an Eights Week in the 1920s, judging from the crowded banks and cheering supporters on the college barges. In 1966, a preservation trust was formed to rescue these elegant barges from total decay but despite this, only a few examples have survived. (*Mary Clarke*)

Looking downstream towards the old lock-house at Iffley, prior to 1924 when the lock was rebuilt. The poplar trees that lined the fringes of the huge pool are still there, which gives some idea of the work involved in draining the pool and constructing the new lock. (*The Environment Agency*)

On 20 May 1908 Iffley Mill, which had been standing since 1170, burnt to the ground in mysterious circumstances. Purchased by Lincoln College in 1445, it was let with the proviso of a free day's fishing annually for the rector and fellows of the college. There are few remains visible today, except for a couple of millstones at the houses nearby. (*Mary Clarke*)

Study of the maps on pages 28 and 29 will show that this photograph was taken in the early 1920s from the Iffley village riverbank looking up the river and across the weir stream; the view today is very different. (*Mary Clarke*)

Lord Desborough, Chairman of the Board of the Thames Conservancy, studies one of the maps outlining the proposed alterations to the river at Iffley in 1923. On 25 July 1885 he was stroke for the crew of an eight that was rowed across the English Channel. (*The Environment Agency*)

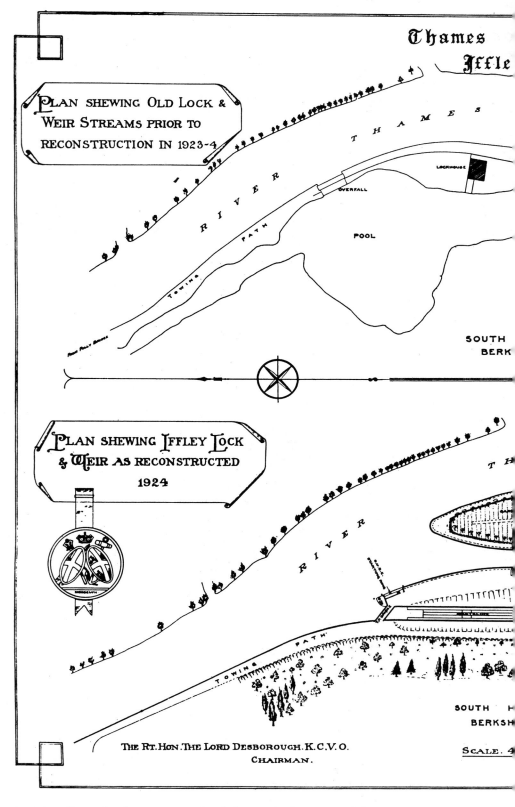

Plan shewing Old Lock & Weir Streams prior to Reconstruction in 1923-4

RIVER THAMES

TOWING PATH

OVERFALL

LOCKHOUSE

POOL

SOUTH BERK

Plan shewing Iffley Lock & Weir as Reconstructed 1924

RIVER

TOWING PATH

SOUTH BERKSH

THE RT. HON. THE LORD DESBOROUGH. K.C.V.O.
CHAIRMAN.

SCALE. 4

Thames
Iffle

An interesting pair of maps comparing before and after views of the river at Iffley in 1923/4. Iffley has the distinction of being one of a trio of locks built in about 1632; the others were at

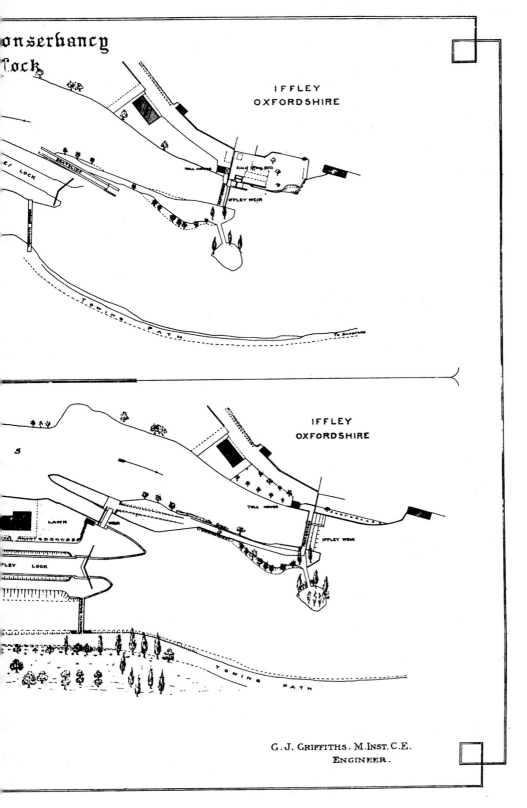

Sandford and Swift Ditch. Some of the original stonework of this lock can still be seen in the weir channel upstream of the weir platform. (*The Environment Agency*)

Looking upstream to Sandford Mill and lock, *c.* 1880. The earlier lock of 1632 can be seen to the left of the mills. This thirteenth-century mill was built by the Knights Templar and has been at the centre of numerous disputes over the years. In about 1370 Oxford bargees were so incensed by delays here that they 'broke down the locks of Sandford' (probably the flash lock of that era). There was a ferry service in operation below the lock dating back to the thirteenth century and a stepped stone used for remounting a horse can still be seen. (*The Environment Agency and The River & Rowing Museum*)

Admittedly this photograph, taken in about 1887, is not one of the best, but it is an important part of Thames history. Swift Ditch lock had the distinction of having the first officially appointed lock-keeper. Appointed by the Second Oxford–Burcot Commission, he was forbidden to marry or sell victuals and lived in a tiny one-up, one-down cottage. Swift Ditch was once the main channel of the Thames and as such it isolated the town of Abingdon. The Abbot of Abingdon did not like this and a deal was struck in the eleventh century with Oxford's wealthy merchants for a new navigation cut. The bizarre cost of using the cut was a toll of herrings – quite how many or how they were obtained is not clear. (*Oxfordshire County Council Photographic Archive*)

2

Swift Ditch Lock to Hart's Lock

Situated in what was once the main navigation channel, the mill at Sutton Courtney has an unusual history. Its existence can be traced back to the late fourteenth century when it was referred to as 'Sutton mylle'. It once had a lock partly under the mill, built around the same time as the locks at Sandford, Iffley and Swift Ditch. The upper mill pool formed part of the lock and as it used a large quantity of water, the miller was able to charge exorbitant tolls to pass through. The levy was said to be the most expensive on the river. The Thames Commissioners received reports that the floor of the mill was causing navigation difficulties and 'frequently hindering the barges there'. Eventually after countless complaints about the tolls and other problems encountered passing through this lock, Culham lock and cut were built in 1809, thus bypassing the mill. This backwater is now a haven of tranquil waters and well worth visiting.

The reach between Benson and Cleeve locks is more than 6 miles of unbroken river. There was once a lock and ferry situated at Chalmore Hole, just below Wallingford. The ferry was established here in about 1788, when the toll for a horse was twopence, but the lock was not built for another fifty years. It was termed a 'summer or low water lock' and only had a small fall of up to 20 inches. By 1883 it had been dismantled completely. Ten years later, in a summer drought, Salter's steamers were unable to run between Wallingford and Oxford because of the shallows below Benson lock and smaller craft were drafted in. There was much local debate and even a call for 'agitation' to be organized for the restoration of Chalmore lock or the building of a new lock at Lower Wharf, Wallingford. Neither happened.

Abingdon lock, 1963. It was here that the author's father, who was lock-keeper at the time, had a close encounter with a rather angry swan. The poor swan in question had become hooked and entangled with fishing line. On a busy Sunday afternoon, a helpful member of the public pointed this out to the lock-keeper who then telephoned the RSPCA, which duly dispatched an officer armed with a bizarre version of a shepherd's crook to help catch the swan. The lock-keeper was pressed into rowing after the hapless bird and, clearly, the swan did not want to be helped. Despite strenuous efforts in the lock punt chasing after this bird, it remained out of reach. The two uniformed men then somehow managed to manoeuvre the swan towards the lock, where members of the public were enjoying the sideshow unfolding before them. The swan, fearing a trap, turned around and, raising a head of steam, shot past the punt. More fruitless chasing ensued with the swan and the lock-keeper becoming increasingly tired. The crowd grew, drawn by the commotion. With one last effort, the RSPCA man managed to hook the bird around the neck and dragged it flapping, squawking and splashing into the punt. The crowd on the lock side clapped and cheered.

Ask anyone about swans and they will tell you that the birds 'can break a man's arm'. This thought was uppermost in the lock-keeper's mind as he leapt upon the bird, wrapping both his arms around the wings in a tight embrace, while the RSPCA officer grappled with the neck of a very angry swan – something akin to wrestling a boa constrictor. Eventually he succeeded in removing the offending hook. At this point the indignant swan was released to tumultuous applause from the crowd. The lock-keeper stood up in the punt and took a bow, to discover that, not only was he covered from head to toe with wet swan's down, but all over his uniform were numerous deposits from the panicked bird! (*Author*)

Abingdon lock, date unknown, showing the old lock-house and the entrance to the backwater surrounding Bushey Eyot, the name given to the land bought in about 1820 by the Commissioners, on which this house stands. Cemented into one of the walls of the current weir is a stone inscribed 'this locke was bvilded by Sir George Stonehovse and Richard Adams Ann 1649'. There was a flash lock situated in this weir and this stone provides some evidence of it. (*Steve Capel-Davies*)

Abingdon Wharf, 1890. With the opening of the Wilts and Berks canal in 1810, and others already taking traffic, Abingdon became a major destination for coal from Wales and the Midlands. Seen here towards the end of its useful life, the wharf at Abingdon had once seen 60-ton barges moor to offload their cargos. A short distance downstream from the wharf was an early version of a fish weir marked on maps as a 'fish gate'. (*Oxfordshire County Council Photographic Archive*)

On a map of 1550 Sutton Courteney Mill is referred to as 'Sutton mylle and Sutton moates'. The 'mylle' had three arches and two gates to one side. The pool seen in this photograph formed part of a lock basin, with the upper gates underneath the mill and the lower gates at the narrowing neck of the pool. The pool used a huge amount of water and the miller charged tolls to match. By 1694 the mill was producing the very first batches of the special paper required by the Bank of England for banknotes. By 1724, because of problems with forgeries, production had moved to Bere Mill near Whitchurch. (*Rural History Centre, University of Reading*)

Looking downstream from Culham lock to Culham Brickyard in 1884. At least one of three kilns on this site close to the Thames is visible. In the foreground are signs of where the clay has been 'won' (dug) from the ground. The four open sheds to the left are called drying hacks and the bricks were left in them for about two weeks prior to firing. To the right bricks are stacked up after being fired in the beehive-shaped kiln behind the cart. On the site today are the well-hidden remains of a vaulted-roofed building, which was possibly part of this operation. (*Oxfordshire County Council Photographic Archive*)

The Thames Conservancy board on their annual inspection at Clifton lock, *c.* 1957. The launch *Windrush* is on the right, *Loddon* on the left and in the background is the *Ember*. Inspections were the bane of the lock-keeper's life and involved lots of work and worry. They ceased in 1968 after seventy years. The lady with her hands on her hips is the author's mother, no doubt berating the board about the lack of proper heating in the lock-house. (*Author*)

The author and his father having fun on the ice in the winter of 1955. Around Clifton lock the meadows often flooded and then froze, providing a reasonably safe environment to venture out on. Jim Goodall was probably dragging us around, as he was a frequent and welcome visitor to the lock. Jim would spend most of his spare time at the lock, helping out with a wide variety of tasks including working on the weir, something that would be frowned upon today. (*Author*)

Some of the author's relatives enjoying the sun in the 1950s at Clifton backwater. The quickest way to the lock was across the backwater from these steps. Occasionally, to supplement his meagre wages as lock-keeper, the author's father would row Midlands anglers across for a day's fishing. Of course, there would be the option of a cup of tea and biscuits available at the lock on arrival. (*Author*)

Leaving Day's lock in the 1930s – before the introduction of speed restrictions on the river! Day's lock has the unusual distinction of having its lock-house built quite some distance away. (*The Warborough and Shillingford History Society*)

Salter's steamer *Marlow* passing under the swing bridge below Day's lock. The people on the bridge appear to be participating in a game of Pooh Sticks, something this bridge is famous for, thanks to retired lock-keeper Lynn David. A staunch supporter of RNLI, Lynn raised many thousands of pounds and was the founder of the International Pooh Sticks Competition held annually at this bridge. He was awarded an OBE for this charity work. (*David Beasley*)

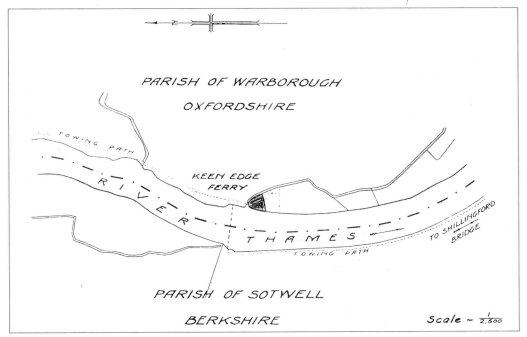

A detailed map of the site of the Keen edge ferry, drawn by the Thames Conservancy surveyor. All of the Conservancy ferries had ceased operation by 1953 but plans are being considered, as this book is written, to build a bridge across the river on the line of the former ferry. (*David Beasley*)

Keen Edge ferry, near Shillingford, 1920s. Where the towpath changed riverbanks, a ferry service had to be provided and this photograph shows examples of the two types of boats used. The smaller punt was used for transporting people across while the larger flat took livestock over, especially horses used for towing. One of the people standing in the flat is a Mrs Bullock from Shillingford. (*The Warborough and Shillingford History Society*)

Keen Edge ferry cottage, 1926. There is little to be seen at this site today because the inlet has been filled in, although some foundations are just about visible. If the scheme to build a bridge here does come to fruition, it will provide a useful link for the long-distance Thames path, avoiding the busy road. (*The Environment Agency*)

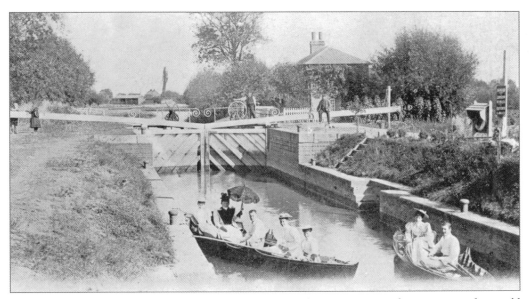

Between the wars postcards were a very effective way of communicating because a sender could dispatch one in the morning telling the recipient that he would be arriving for tea in the afternoon and expect it to get there in time. They were so effective that they were also used by lock-keepers to pass on messages about river levels. The message on the back of this postcard of Benson lock says 'here this morning, no one on the river'. (*Mary Clarke*)

Replacing the lock-gates at Benson, 1930s. It isn't until a photograph such as this appears that one is able to take on board just how massive lock-gates are once they are out of the water. They weigh in at around 80 tons. (*Author*)

The 1929 flood on the River Thames seems to have been forgotten in favour of those in 1894 and 1947, and yet it was almost as bad. This is the walkway across the weir to Benson lock-house, the only way in or out. In the gateway of the weir is the author's grandmother, Florence Eade. The situation must have been quite worrying for her, although one can't help wondering who took the photograph. (*Author*)

Benson ferry, *c.* 1903. In 1912, there were two ferries here, one below the lock and one above. Lock-keepers were often responsible for both the lock and the ferry, and when the author's grandfather was lock-keeper here in the 1930s he operated both. Passengers complained that they were delayed because he didn't always hear them shouting. On the opposite bank to the lock, he installed a bell for passengers to ring when they wanted to cross the river. He later rued doing this, because he could no longer pretend he didn't hear them! (*Hilary Fisher*)

Thomas Bossom owned Wallingford Wharf from 1877 to 1911. After that date timber belonging to merchant Frederick Phillips was stored on the wharf, rather than coal. In the 1894 flood Thomas Bossom was marooned upstairs in the house on the left for several days. The Bossom family also had a boatyard near Port Meadow and had been on the Thames one way or another for more than 200 years. (*David Beasley*)

Harry Grant, aged seventeen, from Warborough, was home on leave in 1942 when the Thames was frozen. After dodging bullets, he needed some fun. First, he checked the thickness of the ice by walking across it and then he cycled on the river. The photograph was taken by Howard Evans. (*David Beasley*)

Percy Turner bought Lower Wharf at Wallingford at the beginning of the twentieth century for boat-building. He later converted the wharf to pleasure uses, including boating and swimming. He is seen here around 1905, teaching his twins John and Eric to swim in a rather unorthodox manner. At the age of two the twins featured in a soap advertisement in a Chicago newspaper and they were renowned for going everywhere barefoot. (*The Warborough and Shillingford History Society*)

A ferry was established at Chalmore Hole in about 1788; Robert Child from Wallingford was the first ferryman. The lock was constructed fifty years later, and both it and the weir were built entirely of timber. By 1881 both gates of the lock were left permanently open and there was no fall at all. Two years later it was dismantled but tolls were still extracted to pass the ruins, much to everyone's annoyance. (*David Beasley*)

This lovely riverside cottage at Chalmore Hole has now disappeared, destroyed by fire. It was the lock-keeper's cottage for the 'summer' or 'low water' lock that once occupied this site. In 1896 the local papers reported a 'block' on the river holding up two fully laden canal boats, an electric launch and a steamer party heading to Wittenham Woods. Complaints were made about the lack of dredging by the Thames Conservancy. (*Ken Townsend*)

Little Stoke ferry, near Moulsford. In 1833 the ferry regulations stated 'that no bargeman, costbearer, owner or other person shall take away or use any ferry boat, at any of the ferries on said navigation, nor any poles or tackle belonging to such ferry without consent and knowledge of the ferryman first obtained'. In less enlightened times the renamed Fair Mile Hospital dominating the horizon in the background was marked on maps as 'Lunatic Asylum'. (*David Beasley*)

This ferry went by many names – South Stoke, Moulsford or Beetle and Wedge – and crossed from South Stoke over to the Beetle and Wedge pub. Whatever its name, it was primarily a horse ferry for transporting towing horses across the river. Just over a mile upstream, the towpath changed banks and yet another ferry was established there to take them back again. This must have been a considerable nuisance for the bargees operating at this time. (*David Beasley*)

The exact date of this photograph is unknown, but it was probably taken in about 1906. Cleeve lock was originally built in 1787 entirely of timber. It had no sides, merely grass banks and beams similar to those in this photograph preventing craft from becoming stuck. Note the lock's name spelt out in stones on the bank. (*The Goring and Streatley Local History Society*)

Cleeve Mill, 1891. With three mills in the area – Cleeve, Goring and Streatley – there was much competition for water and many complaints about obstructions. This was not helped by joint ownership of this mill and Goring mill. During busy times for the millers, they would only shut down for two hours during the night. Believed to have been built in the late sixteenth century, Cleeve was a corn mill with two wheels for grinding; the one remaining wheel now generates some electricity for the holiday apartments here. (*The Goring and Streatley Local History Society*)

Telford Simpson and his boatman aboard the *Hera*, 1903. Mr Simpson once owned The Temple, a large riverside property that has had many famous owners including Rupert Brooke of Brooke-Bond tea and Pete Townsend of the rock group The Who. (*The Goring and Streatley Local History Society*)

The *Hera* moored up at Springfield works, 1903. Sam Saunders started his career in boat-building by making punt poles, he later progressed to punts themselves and then boats at the luxury end of the market, such as this one. The Saunders family business started in about 1830 in the Goring area and later moved to the Isle of Wight. There, they diversified into the manufacture of flying boats and then hovercraft. (*The Goring and Streatley Local History Society*)

The derelict Springfield works, 1970. The boast that punt poles were 'unbreakable' was made by boat-builder Sam Saunders, who once owned these works. Their quality was probably owing to the care and thought that went into seasoning the wood. Each year 100 fir saplings of the required diameter were weighted with chains and sunk near the Swan Hotel. Every third year the same quantity were lifted out and shaped into punt poles which had perfectly seasoned hearts and were therefore 'unbreakable'. (*The Goring and Streatley Local History Society*)

Looking towards Goring Mill, the river and bridge in 1903, when a traction engine was pressed into service to run the electricity generator. The mill was out of action because of the floods seen here. (*The Goring and Streatley Local History Society*)

An unusual photograph of Gatehampton ferry in use in about 1920. The ferryman and probably the horse's owner are taking a horse across the river. Moored at the house in the background is the barge *Penelope*, once owned by Frederick Talbot of Reading. The ferry was established in 1810 and was sometimes referred to as Basildon ferry, possibly because of the proximity of Basildon House. The ferryman's house is still in existence. (*Hilary Fisher*)

The Chiltern Woods end at Hart's lock woods. In the small group of islands below them was a weir described as 'Hart's old wear'. It may have started life as a fish weir, but by 1811 it had fallen into disuse and was partially obstructing the passage. This prompted a report quoted by Thames historian Thacker stating 'Hart's old lock has gone to decay, and is without shutting tackle, but pens a small head of water and causes a shallow below'. (*David Beasley*)

3

Hart's Lock to My Lady Ferry

Referred to in 1802 as 'Hart's old wear', it had already been dismissed as one of the forgotten locks. It was originally thought that this was probably a fishing weir but by 1746 there was nothing left to prevent vessels having free passage through. All that remains of this lock is the name attached to the woods that border the river.

Mapledurham Mill is probably one of the most photographed mills on the Thames. This fine old building went from working order to near collapse and dereliction, but fortunately, timely intervention by conservationists has restored it. Sadly, neither the mill in Caversham's backwaters nor the one at Shiplake have survived; the latter was partly demolished around 1907.

The formidable power of the river in flood has been frequently photographed and well documented. At most locks on the river you will find two flood marks – November 1894 and March 1947. The 1894 flood washed away the bank near Caversham lock and the endless damage and disruption caused by the 1947 flood is still vividly remembered. Improved monitoring and management have largely eliminated this type of event.

With the gradual change to pleasure boating at the beginning of the twentieth century, more and more people ventured out in crafts of all descriptions. Many of these boats and the yards that built them have been lost, although the Thames Traditional Boat Society does much to promote the ownership and use of wooden boats, culminating in their annual rally at Henley in the summer.

The old toll-gate at Whitchurch. Like a great number of Thames bridges, there was a ferry here first. However, unlike most other bridges, the current steel construction is only the third on this site – most sites had many more. Built in about 1902 to replace the two previous wooden bridges, Whitchurch shares the distinction of still being a toll-bridge with the one at Eynsham. (*Hilary Fisher*)

Mapledurham mill, photographed before 1922, is the last working mill on the River Thames and was mentioned in Domesday Book. In 1677 the mill had two waterwheels that turned four pairs of stones. In later years more expansion followed with the building of a storage barn and a wharf from which flour, crushed oats and bran were sent by barge to London. The 1976 film *The Eagle has Landed* starring Michael Caine, Donald Sutherland and Robert Duvall was filmed here. A complete village was constructed around the existing buildings and the location fee from the film funded the restoration of the mill. In the film, Mapledurham's mill wheel played a gruesome part in the death of a German soldier. (*Graham Parlour*)

Mapledurham ferry has also been called Purley and there was another ferry in close proximity downstream named Roebuck after the inn of the same name. These two ferries owed their existence to the stubbornness of one man, Mr Worlidge, who steadfastly refused to allow a towpath over his land, and so in the space of half a mile the towpath crossed the river twice. (*Hilary Fisher*)

Weed clearing in the backwater behind Caversham lock. In the background is Caversham Mill. It was mentioned in Domesday Book and was once a corn mill, producing flour for the biscuit trade. Part of the mechanism of the mill is still there today. (*Graham Parlour*)

Caversham Bridge, photographed before 1869 when a continuous iron bridge was built; this picture shows a half-timber, half-stone bridge. Because of a dispute between the two counties, the Berkshire side was made of timber, while the Oxfordshire side was the stone portion. There was a chapel here to which pilgrims made their way, donating alms that went towards the upkeep of the bridge. Records are unclear when this bridge was built, but it was probably one of the oldest on the river, dating from somewhere between 1163 and 1231. (*Graham Parlour*)

Swimming in the river was popular between the wars and many bathing places were set up to cater for this. At Reading there were two, and this photograph shows Cawston's lido, which featured diving boards and even a deep end. The popularity of the bathing places waned with the opening of council swimming pools. (*Graham Parlour*)

The Thames in flood, 1894. Here the river has breached the towpath at Caversham lock. The photograph was taken looking downstream and the view is almost unrecognizable today. (*The Environment Agency*)

Caversham weir in flood on 16 March 1947. The weir 'runners' or 'gang' placed themselves in extreme danger in order to keep the weir clear of debris; a blockage at this time would have had a dramatic effect on the level of the river, causing even more flooding. There is little doubt that a slip would have had fatal consequences. (*The Environment Agency*)

Before regulations were introduced restricting the number of passengers that vessels were allowed to carry, scenes such as this were commonplace. In Caversham lock, the steamer *River Queen* has a party of Catholic school children aboard and a band; together they total at least 112 people! Problems of overcrowding still occur today, especially during regatta week at Henley. (*Graham Parlour*)

The Thames Conservancy launch *Loddon* passing Caversham church on patrol in the 1930s. The launches were named after Thames tributaries, although another – *Donola* – had to have its name changed from *Lodona* to avoid confusion with this boat. (*Graham Parlour*)

Near Reading, June 1903. This foolish attempt to discover the limit of the towpath would have had more serious consequences if the edge had been found. (*Graham Parlour*)

Sonning lock, *c.* 1900. Most lock-houses have two flood marks affixed to the wall, 1894 and 1947. Generally, though not always, they also have the date the house was built on the gable, in this case 1916. One lady boater expressed surprise at the height of the 1916 floods! (*The Environment Agency and The River & Rowing Museum*)

Making a pleasant change from the usual picturesque view of Sonning Bridge, here is a view taken in 1901 of part of the bridge that once led over to the mill here. A flat is being positioned for 'bucket and spoon' dredging, the mechanism clearly visible towards the bow of the boat. (*Rural History Centre, University of Reading*)

There has been summer camping on Shiplake island since 1889 when it was purchased by the City of London. Handed down from generation to generation, each plot was furnished with wooden decking upon which huge tents were pitched for the summer. Despite new attempts to purchase the island, this practice continues today, perhaps with more modern versions of the barbecue seen near the riverbank. (*Hilary Fisher*)

Shiplake mill before 1907 when it was partially demolished. Much loved by artists and photographers, it was referred to before Domesday. It was owned by the prioress of Goring in 1404. By 1790, it may have been owned by Mr Cotterell, possibly the same man who looked after Shiplake lock. (*Hilary Fisher*)

The commencement of the building of the River & Rowing Museum on Mill Meadows at Henley, showing the building's foundation piles. Because of the site's proximity to the Thames, these piles were deemed necessary to protect the building in case of floods. (*Christopher Cove-Smith*)

A few months later and the museum's ground-floor platforms are in place. The photograph was taken looking towards the river and the tall poplar trees in the background very effectively screen the building from the Thames. (*Christopher Cove-Smith*)

A stunning exterior photograph of the completed museum, showing architect David Chipperfield's boathouse-inspired vision. Formally opened by HRH Queen Elizabeth in November 1998, this independent museum celebrates three themes: the River Thames, the town of Henley on Thames and the international sport of rowing. In 1999, it was designated Royal Fine Arts Commission Building of the Year and was Museum of the Year 1999–2000. (*Jaap Oepkes*)

Inside the museum's Thames gallery with the elegant *Flierefluiter* in the foreground. The largest of the museum's three galleries features a journey down the Thames from source to sea. Along the way, displays explore the many facets of the river from history, archaeology and ecology, to water management and conservation. (*Jaap Oepkes*)

A close-up image of the mills near Marsh lock. There were two mills here, one on the Berkshire bank and one on the Oxfordshire side. At one time or another both have been confusingly referred to as 'new', although the mill on the Oxfordshire side is the real 'new' mill, dating back to 1585. (*Mary Clarke*)

Photographed by Marsh brothers, who appeared in local trade directories up until 1904, this unusual shot of Henley Bridge looks downstream to Fawley Court, just visible in the distance. The large sheds in the middle distance formed part of Webb's Wharf which once stretched from New Street to the edge of Phyllis Court. They were demolished in 1886 and replaced by boathouses and other properties at the end of Wharf Lane. (*Hilary Fisher*)

Henley Regatta has always been a popular event and never more so than in the 1920s when this photograph was taken. At certain times it was possible to cross the river by stepping in and out of the various boats on the water. In the foreground is a man holding a sign appealing for £50,000 for the Berkshire Hospital. (*John Cook*)

The crowded riverbank during Henley regatta, possibly near Fawley meadows, in the early 1900s. Each year the Thames Traditional Boat Society brings its lovingly restored wooden boats to Henley for a rally. Fashions such as those seen here are not compulsory but they do add to the sense of occasion. (*Hilary Fisher*)

The houseboat *Rouge et Noir* at Henley, probably in the 1920s and almost certainly moored for the duration of the regatta. A fine example of Victorian overkill, the view of the rowing from the upper deck of this boat would have been superb. Some wealthy owners would even hire orchestras from London to entertain their guests aboard these houseboats. Of course, the less well off would simply paddle up and down in their boats and be entertained for nothing. (*Hilary Fisher*)

Before Hambledon became a pound lock in about 1773, like others of that time it was a flash lock and bargees were obliged to winch their craft upstream on the flash of released water. The winch behind the lock-house survived until at least 1881. In the fourteenth century two men were mortally wounded when the cable violently parted company from the 'landwynch' that held it. (*Hilary Fisher*)

A wide variety of motor cars drive across a pontoon bridge near Aston ferry, early 1900s. Many of these bridges were built as exercises for the army. The longest known pontoon bridge on the Thames was erected between Gravesend and Tilbury. (*Hilary Fisher*)

Aston ferry started life as a rope ferry in about 1785. A rope was stretched across the river to pull the ferryboat across, but this was a hazard to other boats and in this photograph (probably taken in the 1930s) a chain, which ran along the riverbed, has replaced the rope. The ferryman is seen taking two horses, their riders and dogs across the river, although the dogs may have belonged to the ferryman. (*Mary Clarke*)

Although the exact location of The Ferry Tea Boat has not been determined, it is quite possible that E. Wuytack ran it from a spot close to the Henley Regatta. (*Graham Parlour*)

Taken by the same photographer as the Temple lock picture at the top of the opposite page, this view amply portrays the timeless elegance of river parties at the beginning of the twentieth century. Although the location is not known for certain, it may have been one of the numerous backwaters around Hurley. (*Joe Green*)

A rowing or gentlemen's club. This photograph was probably taken before 1890 when Temple lock was replaced by the current lock built alongside. Despite enhancement possible with modern technology, the lock-keeper's name on the sign above the door remains elusive, but it could be F.S. Jones who was lock-keeper here from 1884 to 1886. Note that the man on the right moved while the picture was being taken and his face has been retouched. Yet the two dogs managed to remain still! (*Joe Green*)

The Siren photographed in about 1889 from the riverbank opposite Higginson Park at Marlow. The old boathouse can be seen in the centre of the view. (*Joe Green*)

Marlow Bridge and church, looking downstream, *c.* 1889. All along this side of the river at Marlow there were many wharves, including those for coal and timber. Supposedly belonging to Bisham Abbey, 'The Barn' (seen to the left of the bridge) was thought to be a tithe barn. It was later demolished and replaced by a boatyard, which in turn was replaced by the riverside flats we see today. (*The Marlow Society*)

Every year Marlow amateur regatta draws entrants from around the world. It is considered by some to be a warm up for the main event at Henley. Not all races are taken too seriously, as this photograph from the 1930s of a canoe race starting at Marlow Bridge and drawing large crowds shows. Note the third canoe from the right is about to capsize. (*Ken Townsend*)

Marlow Mills and lock, 1890. These mills were later to produce corn, paper, thimbles and 'oyle'. They were demolished in 1965 and two years later the houses currently occupying the site were built in a similar style to the old clapper-boarded mill. They went on the market priced between £16,000 and £18,000; one local resident was heard to remark 'They'll never sell at that price' and they did remain unsold for some time. One can only speculate what they might be worth today. (*The Environment Agency and The River & Rowing Museum*)

St Peter Street floods, Marlow, looking towards the river, 1894. This street was once called Duck Lane, because of the presence of the town's ducking stool. It led to the early wooden bridge that crossed here but is now a public slipway. One chap lost his way in Marlow in the early hours and sped down this street thinking that it left town; realizing his error too late, he drove full tilt into the river. His momentum took him right across to the weir, where his car sank. Extricating himself from the car and clambering on to the weir platform, he ran to the lock-house and knocked frantically on the door. Dripping wet, he announced to the sleepy lock-keeper that he had driven his car into the river. The lock-keeper's initial thoughts were 'Why are you telling me this?' Once the reason was explained, the lock-keeper became calmer and idly wondered whether the car was a Ford! (*David Wilson*)

'Three men in a boat' below Marlow lock around the beginning of the twentieth century. In the background are Quarry Woods, once a favourite haunt for picnic parties. Slightly further downstream from here was the now defunct Riverside ferry which crossed the river to Winter Hill, a local landmark. (*Joe Green*)

Spade Oak ferry was established in about 1822 on the site of a former wharf owned by Mr Rose, who in earlier times exercised a right to tow barges along from his land and up to Marlow, making a charge for this service. This Thames Conservancy ferry was still operational up until the mid-1950s, when it was finally closed. (*Ken Townsend*)

The rather sombre occasion of a ferry punt being used as a hearse to ferry the coffin of Mr Lysip across the river in the 1930s. The floods did not make the journey any easier for Eric, Norman, Rob and Les Townsend, who were given the task of paddling the boat across under the watchful eye of their father Ernest and the undertaker. (*Ken Townsend*)

The Bourne End Regatta, 1906. This event was originally held to celebrate the golden jubilee of Queen Victoria in 1887. In the background of the photograph is Townsend's boatyard which was founded in 1884 by Robert Townsend after he acquired the redundant wharf known as Wiggington's coal yard. Here boats of every type were built including skiffs, dinghies, canoes, punts and sailing vessels. Thriving until the 1960s, the boatyard was sold to Tom Jones and is now a marina. (*Ken Townsend*)

Stan Townsend, the owner of Townsend's boatyard at Bourne End, poles passengers across the river for a halfpenny each in 1937. During the course of one August bank holiday, the ferry took an astonishing 3,500 people in *each* direction in one day. A busy, tiring and yet rewarding weekend. (*Ken Townsend*)

My Lady ferry, Cookham, was one of the many operating in the area. In the background of the photograph is the picturesque ferryman's cottage, now available for holiday rental from the National Trust. (*Ken Townsend*)

4

My Lady Ferry to Eel Pie Island

At Cookham there is ample opportunity to misinterpret information about the numerous ferries that once operated in the area. Four were indicated on a map dated 1912, although official names for only three can be found. They were: Upper, Lower (variously called Middle, Hedsor and Cliveden) and My Lady. According to Thames historian Fred Thacker, My Lady was said to be a corruption of Islade or Islake, the name given to one of several royal fisheries in the area, although there was also a meadow here called Lady Mead, which could have lent its name to this ferry.

Boulter's lock, near Maidenhead, was one of the river's busiest locks and was immortalized in Edward Gregory's famous painting. Boulter's lock on Ascot Sunday was once the place to see and be seen, the lockside teeming with people peering down at boaters peering up.

For over 600 years the London Stone at Staines demarcated the City of London's upper limit of jurisdiction over the Thames and each year the Mayor and his entourage journeyed up the river to the stone. Here a loyal toast was drunk – 'God preserve the City of London' – and money was strewn among the crowd. Unfortunately, this ancient ceremony degenerated into official horseplay with the Mayor being bumped rather unceremoniously.

Walton-on-Thames has had its fair share of bridges and it is frequently alleged that Julius Caesar crossed here at Cowey Sale. Although most references to the first bridge built here date from around 1750, repairs to a bridge are referred to in the quarter sessions order book of 1662 – perhaps this was really the first one on the site.

As far as is known, the ferry at Twickenham was established in about 1659 as an accommodation ferry, carrying only passengers (as opposed to a navigation ferry which carried horses, etc.). In 1908, when a rival ferry run by Hammerton and Messum set up in competition nearby, the owner of Twickenham ferry, the Earl of Dysart, took them to court, finally losing his case in the House of Lords six years later. Numerous ferries that once plied their trade across the Thames have gone.

In 1901 the Mayor of Maidenhead, William Ferguson Good, and his entourage set about the perambulation of the borough, calling at various points along the way. Here they are seen just above Maidenhead Bridge in a punt, having travelled part of the way by steamer. (© *Royal Borough Museum Collection*)

William Ferguson Good provided a fine example of Newton's third law, which states that for every action there is an equal and opposite reaction.
He managed to fall in when stepping from a punt in 1901, an incident inevitably captured for posterity by a photographer. (© *Royal Borough Museum Collection*)

Bourne End, Marlow and Cookham units of the Upper Thames Patrol (UTP) on joint exercise in the Cliveden reach, early 1940s. Formed as a waterborne version of 'Dad's Army', the UTP was crewed entirely by volunteers and lock-keepers and their brief was observation, communication and intelligence. Initially they had little in the way of uniform or weapons but later they were issued with full Home Guard uniform. However, they retained their distinctive UTP badges and shoulder flashes. Although the UTP may not have been involved in direct conflict, its members were able to help the war effort in many other ways, such as guarding bridges, carrying out searches, disabling boats to prevent enemy use and patrolling the river as seen here. (*Ken Townsend*)

Locks on the Thames have provided perpetual fascination for the public, none more so than Boulter's, where the lock is so accessible. This superb photograph captures the colourful gaiety and crowded chaos of a busy day at the lock, *c.* 1900. (*Rural History Centre, University of Reading*)

After months of rain and snow, the thaw set in and one of the most famous Thames floods occurred in 1947. Here, outside the Magpie Hotel in Windsor, the army and a 'duck' helped to rescue people worst hit by the catastrophe. (*The Environment Agency*)

Eton upper boats and *Britannia* in Boveney lock, 1885. The upper boats were rowed by senior boys and, conversely, the lower boats were crewed by lower boys. Eton boys were encouraged to venture upstream and the earliest account of this taking place dates from 1793. This practice was not officially allowed until 1840, when Dr Hawtrey 'legalized' boating activities. (*By permission of the Provost and Fellows of Eton College*)

Bray lock, *c.* 1890, shortly after it was rebuilt. Originally this lock had no sides, only turf banks and rubbing strakes to stop vessels becoming stuck. A lock-keeper was once interrupted here by an evening phone call during his favourite comedy show. The caller voiced concern about a water bird in his garden and the keeper asked him to describe it. The line went quiet and some minutes later the caller returned to say the bird had a green head. Having just received a description of a mallard duck, the keeper decided to make his own comedy as he was missing the jokes on television. He asked the man if the bird had a white ring around his neck: more silence while the caller went to check. The man then returned to confirm the presence of a white ring, whereupon the lock-keeper told him not to worry as this bird was known as the 'Vicar of Bray' and if he stopped feeding him he would just fly away. As the keeper returned to his lounge, the programme finished. His wife said that he had just missed a good laugh. 'Snap', replied the lock-keeper! (*The Environment Agency and The River & Rowing Museum*)

Windsor Castle, *c.* 1880. This looks like a backwater rather than the main channel of the Thames. Built by William the Conqueror over 900 years ago, the castle was originally intended as defence for the western approach to London. Improved upon by each successive monarch, this is the largest castle continually occupied by members of the royal family. (© *Royal Borough Museum Collection*)

Queen Victoria's silver jubilee in 1862 was celebrated with the ceremonial procession seen here. The bridge leading towards Windsor Castle was decorated with a triumphal arch made of painted canvas and wood and adorned with the words 'God save the Queen'. (© *Royal Borough Museum Collection*)

The dangerous practice of venturing out on to a frozen river, 1891. One would have to be very certain that the river was well and truly frozen before doing this. (© *Royal Borough Museum Collection*)

Windsor Castle photographed from the Brocas, *c.* 1910. The word Brocas is believed to mean a wood near a castle. The wooded island in the centre of the view is Firework Ait and a ferry service once operated nearby. (*Alan Beaven*)

King Stable Street, Eton, suffering from rising water, 1894. In the foreground on the right is the butchers shop of Webb & Son. Note the meat hanging to the left of the doorway. On the left of the photograph the bakers in their white caps look out of their doorway. Both of these buildings still stand, as well as a few of the terraced houses. (© *Royal Borough Museum Collection*)

The Fourth of June procession of boats adjacent to Romney lock at the beginning of the twentieth century. King George III had a particular fondness for Eton and the boys celebrated his birthday on 4 June with boat processions. Standing up in a 'longboat' (a clinker-built eight) would have been a difficult feat to achieve without a superb sense of balance. (© *Royal Borough Museum Collection*)

Romney lock with Windsor Castle shrouded in mist in the background, 1890. Opened to traffic in 1797, Romney lock seems to have acquired its name as a corruption of Rumley, a man who ten years earlier owned part of the towpath near here. (*The Environment Agency and The River & Rowing Museum*)

Roger French, Brian Lapworth and David Cunningham avoiding tolls at Romney lock in 1955 by portaging their canoes across the overspill of the weir. Note the swan feather in the hat of one of the boys and the 1930s canvas-covered canoe. (*Roger French*)

A busy day at Bell Weir lock, probably in the late 1920s. Each boat had a name and the lock-keeper was required to log every one of them in a book, collect tolls, help with ropes, as well as winding the sluices and pushing the lock beams. (*Martin Adams*)

Thames Conservancy.

PLEASURE BOAT TOLLS.

No. 865

BELL WEIR LOCK

Received for the passage of a Pleasure Boat "ONCE through, by, or over, and returning on the same day."

SIXPENCE.

Dated..194........

N.B.—All persons passing through this Lock in or with a Steam, Electric or Petrol Motor Launch, are required to receive a Ticket with the date filled up in writing, and to produce the same when requested.

All persons using the River Thames, and the Locks, Works and Towing Paths thereof, do so at their own risk, and must take them as they find them.

SEE BACK

NOT TRANSFERABLE.

A toll ticket from Bell Weir lock. These tickets were once commonly issued to craft for passage through the various locks, a practice that eventually ceased in 1967. Collecting the money from small boats required the use of a long pole with a canvas bag with eyelets attached. Great care was needed collecting tolls with this pole for obvious reasons. (*Martin Adams*)

The Angler's Rest pub near Bell weir lock after the fire of 1911. This pub was particularly popular with one of the summer lock assistants, Freddy Mills. After a lunchtime session he returned to the lock the worse for drink. For helping a boater tie up he was given a bottle of ale as a reward and upon taking it, promptly fell in the lock and went under. He was renowned for his affection for ale, so no one was surprised when he was pulled out of the water tightly clutching the bottle of beer! The Runnymede Hotel is now on the site of the pub. (*The Egham Museum Trust*)

Staines Bridge around the turn of the twentieth century with the Swan Hotel boathouse in the background. Staines has had at least five bridges spanning the river, from the early versions built with tree trunks, to those of iron and wood and eventually the more elegant (and longer-lasting) granite construction built by Rennie. Part of the 1791 stone bridge, which collapsed after only two years, is still just visible on the Surrey towpath side. The two barges seen here, *Elizabeth* on the right and *Swan* at the back, were owned by E. Timmins of Staines. (*Andy McGrandle*)

Looking north towards Staines Bridge, 1949. The temporary bridge upstream was erected during the Second World War in case the main bridge was bombed. In the centre of the view is the emerging roundabout. On both sides of the road in the foreground are the buildings for Lagonda Cars, later to merge with Aston Martin. (Lagonda is an Indian name meaning buck's horns.) (*The Egham Museum Trust*)

The enigmatic 'Fishing Temple' photographed from the river, *c.* 1900. It was known as Fisher House in 1770; however, a map of 1761 uses the former title. It is thought that it may have some connection with the ancient Savory's weir nearby. Often weirs were set up primarily to trap or catch fish and this 'temple' may well have been home to early fishermen (perhaps they prayed for a good catch!). Later it was used both as a coaling wharf and a charging station for Immisch's electric launches. Unfortunately, caravans surround it today. (*Andy McGrandle*)

Penton Hook lock is barely recognizable in this view from the beginning of the twentieth century. It was here that the local postman gave himself a fright one day when he forgot to put the handbrake on in his van. When he looked round, the van was rolling backwards towards the river. Without thinking he jumped into the vehicle, despite the fact that he couldn't swim. The van shot past a fisherman, narrowly missing him, and plunged into the river. Fortunately the fisherman knew that although the front of the van was completely under water, the back was in only 6 ft. The fisherman calmly told the postman to jump out the back and all would be well. At that time the lock-keeper arrived with the local policeman and all they could do was laugh. The postman survived his ordeal, the van was recovered and the post dried, sorted and forwarded to its destination, albeit 'watermarked'. (*Rural History Centre, University of Reading*)

Look at a map of the Thames in this area and you will find the Abbey river coming down from the bends at Penton Hook. Also known as Oxley Mill river, it is probable that this watercourse was cut by monks to turn the wheels of the mill seen here. Dating back to at least the eleventh century, the huge monastery was built on the island known as Cerotsey which is formed by the Thames and the Abbey river. (*The Environment Agency and The River & Rowing Museum*)

Beer barrel racing, possibly at Weybridge Regatta, 3 March 1912. Beer barrel racing was just one of many novelty events staged at amateur regattas. Along with walking the greasy pole, this would have been tricky to master – too fast and you are sunk, paddle slowly and the race is lost. (*The Egham Museum Trust*)

Taken outside Weybridge Ladies Amateur Rowing Club, this photograph brilliantly captures that winning feeling and is included in this book on the strength of that alone. It is therefore unfortunate that little is known about why these ladies were celebrating or the date of the picture. (*The River & Rowing Museum*)

The tank 'Alecto' forges its way through 3 ft of floodwater approaching Shepperton High Street in 1947. 'Alecto' was an experimental tank built by Vickers Armstrong at Chertsey for the Ministry of Defence. On this occasion it was being used to transport Roy Buller, Bob Delacy, G. Faulkner, Eric Jones, Ernie Mansfield, Dave Morgan, Don Tyler, and an unknown lady to work. During the day it was also used to deliver milk and bread to homes cut off by floodwater. (*G. Faulkner*)

Between the Red Lion and the Ship Hotel at Shepperton, the riverbank was known as 'The Shore' and two ferries, Rosewell's and Purdue's, operated from here in fierce competition, especially during regatta time. Russell Rosewell's ferry charged a penny fare and he would often take up to ten people across at a time. (*Sunbury and Shepperton Local History Society*)

Halliford bends and George Purdue's boatshed near Ferry Square, *c.* 1900. The name Purdue was associated with a ferry here as early as the fifteenth century. Later members of the Purdue family may have been fishermen in Shepperton from the eighteenth century, developing this business where you could have your 'boats taken care of and housed for the season'. (*Andy McGrandle*)

In the 1920s Shepperton ferry was often called Dunton's after the family who owned and operated both it and the boatyard. The building on the island in the background is Eyot House, built by Richard D'Oyly Carte of the Savoy Opera Company in the 1890s. Many opera stars would gather in the evenings for rehearsals and their performances could be heard quite clearly nearby. Sailing away from the ferry is the steamer *Britannia*, built in 1894 by Maynard's of Reading. (*Sunbury and Shepperton Local History Society*)

Dunton's ferry, Shepperton. Boats were 'let by hour or day' from the building on the right. To the left is the riverside café where one could have either a tea party or a beanfeast. George Dunton owned and operated this ferry in addition to building boats, punts and canoes. (*John Cook*)

Looking towards the area known locally as Windmill Green from Walton Bridge, November 1894. To visualize this location today, note that Walton Lane bears left to Shepperton while Walton Bridge Road heads right with the garage on the corner. Two enterprising locals are ready with their punts to help people stranded by the flood and in the centre of the view is a Thames Valley Dairy milk cart. (*Nick Pollard*)

Walton Bridge from the air, 1919. This photograph shows just how much development has taken place in a relatively short space of time. There was once a timber wharf on the Walton side upstream from the bridge; the barge rubbing posts are just visible close to the track alongside the river. (*Walton Library*)

Rosewell's boathouse just downstream from Walton Bridge, probably photographed in the 1920s judging by the clothes of the gentleman in the foreground. The building has hardly altered and is part of the marina now situated in the backwater. (*Walton Library*)

The backwater downstream of Walton Bridge, known as Walton Sea. Study of a Thames map of this area reveals an extremely large lake between Weybridge and Walton. Broadwater Lake has the hallmarks of an oxbow lake. Perhaps the original course of the River Thames ran through this lake and into the backwater. (*Walton Library*)

The bridges at Walton-on-Thames looking upstream would be barely recognizable today by comparison with this view taken before the Second World War. Across the marshy ground to the left is the approach causeway built for the 1780 bridge. To the right is the bridge built in 1864. Although this was, and still is, an important place to cross the river, all of the bridges that have crossed here have been inadequate for one reason or another. (*Walton Library*)

The Anglers and the Swan Hotel at Walton-on-Thames, captured by Oxford photographer Henry Taunt *c.* 1898. At this time, Jason Gurney & Co. ran the Anglers pub. In the background several men are unloading coal from barges into a cart to supply the local gasworks. Between these two pubs were the boat-building premises of B. Harris. The sheds occupied by this business have now become an art gallery. (*The Environment Agency*)

Looking downstream to the old Sunbury lock, certainly photographed before 1926, when a new lock was built alongside. The lock-house in this view was demolished in 1959 and a few years ago during some garden work the building plaque from the house was discovered. Restored and painted, it may be seen today beside the old lock. (*Sunbury and Shepperton Local History Society*)

The old wharf in the backwater at Lower Sunbury, 1920s. The wharf was silted up by 1897, falling into disuse as a result of this and the reduction in barge traffic. In the eighteenth and nineteenth centuries it was busy and was known as Church wharf. It was located near Wilson's ferry, which was run by the local boatyard owner. The house in the background is Weir View, which was demolished in 1962. (*Sunbury and Shepperton Local History Society*)

Sunbury, or Clarke's ferry as it was often called after the family that ran it. A ferry was mentioned here as early as 1604 and it is possible that it crossed in the same place. The ferry house has since been replaced with a bungalow. (*Sunbury and Shepperton Local History Society*)

Hampton ferry, photographed in the 1930s, has been carrying passengers almost without a break since 1514 and the horse races held at Hurst Park since the 1700s certainly contributed to its popularity. A story is told that the large ferry flat was so tightly packed during race weekends that passengers on the outside linked arms in order to stay on board. (*John Cook*)

The ferry taking pleasure-seekers across to the 'Karsino' on Tagg's Island in the 1920s. Fred Westcott was once a busker at Molesey lock. He changed his name to Fred Karno and invented the custard-pie-in-the-face routine. He later made his fortune from Fred Karno's Circus. With this fortune he built the 'Karsino', which was opened on Sunday 18 May 1913 with 5,000 people in attendance. (*John Cook*)

When Fred Karno decided to build this hotel, he envisaged a 'sumptuous palace'. He was true to his vision, for the finished complex included a restaurant, bar, hotel, ballroom, six lawn tennis courts, a theatre and the Palm Court, which could seat 800 people to listen to the resident orchestra. Despite several aborted attempts to revive this hotel, it was demolished in 1971. (*London Borough of Richmond upon Thames, Local Studies Collection*)

Molesey lock, *c.* 1897. In 1834 a licensed waterman was rowing a party of two ladies with their babies and maids down to Kingston when the boat became caught in the gates of this lock. With the water rising rapidly, the ladies panicked and in desperation, resorted to throwing their babies out on to the bank and then scrambling to safety themselves. The lock-keeper at the time, Mr Peart, successfully claimed that he was not responsible for the safety of pleasure vessels as they did not pay a toll! (*Andy McGrandle*)

Photographed before 1864, the second wooden bridge at Hampton Court was built at a cost of nearly £7,000 between 1776 and 1788 when it was finally opened to traffic. This bridge was demolished in 1864 and replaced by a cast-iron one, which in turn was replaced by the current bridge in 1933, although slightly downstream from the original crossings. (*Elmbridge Museum, Weybridge*)

Looking upstream to the cast-iron Hampton Court Bridge and the Castle Hotel, probably *c.* 1900. Note the coal barge and the profusion of skiffs and punts. (*Andy McGrandle*)

Hampton Court Bridge in the 1920s, looking towards Molesey. Closest to the bridge on the right was Nuttalls Hotel and restaurant. Nearer to the camera was the Palace Gate restaurant and on the corner, a sweet shop. The view today is far more chaotic with a roundabout and a great deal of traffic. (*Gillian Goodbright*)

Aerial view of the construction of the new Hampton Court Bridge, *c.* 1933. At the same time just downstream of the bridge the river was widened and dredged, and the banks re-profiled. (*The Environment Agency*)

After the building of Hampton Court's fourth bridge, the tricky task of dismantling the large cast-iron posts began. It was undertaken by the firm of Mowlem & Co. Ltd. (*The Environment Agency*)

Kingston photographed from the Parade with barges *Prosperous* and *Ernest* moored in front of a sunken houseboat, *c.* 1900. The word 'Ferry' is visible, painted on the wall to the right of the photograph; however, no record of this ferry can be found. (*Andy McGrandle*)

A very early view taken from Kingston Bridge looking downstream towards the railway bridge. One of the former bridges here boasted a ducking stool for nagging wives; it ducked them into the water 'over the hed and eres'. (*The Environment Agency*)

'I say, old bean, have you caught anything yet?' 'No such luck, old chap. Fish are jolly well not biting, what?' Two 'toffs' fishing on Teddington weir in their top hats! (*London Borough of Richmond upon Thames, Local Studies Collection*)

'Ahoy! and Oho, and it's who's for the ferry?' (The briar's in bud and the sun's going down:) And I'll row ye so quick and I'll row ye so steady, And 'tis but a penny to Twickenham Town.' Twickenham ferryman and passenger, 1890. (*London Borough of Richmond upon Thames, Local Studies Collection*)

Mr and Mrs Harry Knight Milham with their daughter Connie and Fluff the dog aboard one of two gondolas built by Mr Milham for the river pageant celebrating Twickenham's gaining borough status in 1926. Mr Milham hired a gondolier from Venice especially for the occasion. (*Gordon Shilleto*)

Swan Island, 1932. It was originally known as Milham's Ait after Harry Knight Milham, the man who built the island out of clay excavated during the construction of London Underground's Central line. An outstanding pioneer, Milham helped build the fuselage of the First World War Sopwith as well as the hull of one of the first boats powered by an aero engine. In 1905 he took out a patent on the first fully reversible aircraft propeller. But he was primarily a boat-builder and he founded Ferry works for that purpose, employing many craftsmen. At his boatyard he built *Elizabeth Green*, one of the boats used for the evacuation of Dunkirk. A testament to his skills, she is still afloat today. (*Gordon Shilleto*)

An immaculately composed early twentieth-century photograph of Twickenham from the ferry, with possibly the ferry punt in the centre of the view. Note the two barges and steam boat in the distance. (*London Borough of Richmond upon Thames, Local Studies Collection*)

Eel Pie island near Twickenham. It is thought that the island was once the site of a monastery. Henry VIII is said to have frequented the island for courtship (for 'courtship', read seduction or worse). In later years it was host to early British rhythm and blues at the Island Hotel, featuring, among others, John Mayall and Alexis Korner. (*London Borough of Richmond upon Thames, Local Studies Collection*)

A local fisherman with his catch on Boxing Day, 1935. The eel weighed in at 3 lb and was at least 3 ft long. Probably a female, as they tend to grow longer than the males, this specimen was caught by Ted Ryall, a member of the local angling club. Members would fish every Sunday during the season and then retire to 'The Barmy Arms' to quench their thirst. Later after a few drinks, they would probably alter the weight and length of their catch! (*Barbara Chilton*)

5

Eel Pie Island to the Sea

One can only speculate how Eel Pie Island came to get its name, but there was once a tavern on the island where eel pies were served and perhaps it is derived from this.

One of the early trades practised on the Thames was the cultivation of willow trees for commercial use. Osier rods from these trees were in constant demand. Professional fishermen needed fish and eel traps made from them and they had numerous other applications, including baskets, containers and even riverbank reinforcements. Most of the commercial growing took place on the numerous aits or islands on the Thames because of the high quality of the soil there.

London's dock system was once the envy of the world, with a rich diversity of goods arriving and departing daily. Docklands became known, too, as a 'thieves kitchen': an estimated half a million pounds worth of goods were lost annually in the eighteenth century. The various owners and operators were clearly not going to tolerate these losses and this led to the formation of the oldest police force in the world at Wapping.

After passing the docks and heading out into the estuary, one could be forgiven for thinking the marshy areas of London have little to offer us in terms of history. Yet around Tilbury and Gravesend there remains evidence of estuary defences, including two forts and the remains of a battery built during the reign of Henry VIII, the foundations of which are still visible.

More recent defences for the Thames estuary were built shortly after the evacuation of Dunkirk in 1940. There were two distinct designs for these so-called 'secret forts'. Their purpose was the same – to protect and defend the estuary and London from airborne attack.

When the new London Bridge was built, along with numerous wharves and embankments, the tidal reaches of the Thames were seriously affected. High tides became higher and low tides lower. A marked increase in housing development led to a rise in the discharges of effluent into the river. At low tides the stench was awful and this led to the proposal to build Richmond half-tide lock and weir. This photograph shows the start of construction, seen from the Surrey side in 1892. The project was completed by 1894 for the official opening by the Duke of York on 17 May. The final structure was deemed to be a success and happily coincided with a boom in recreational activities on the river. (*London Borough of Richmond upon Thames, Local Studies Collection*)

Photographed in 1894, F. Stoney, the inventor and patent holder of the sluice design for Richmond half-tide lock. He was known as one of 'The Worthies'. (*Richmond Local History Society*)

The start of the 'Through London' swimming contest, Richmond lock. The race was 14½ miles from Richmond to HMS *Buzzard* near Blackfriars Bridge. There were thirty-seven starters, including six ladies, but only eighteen managed to complete the full distance. (*London Borough of Richmond upon Thames, Local Studies Collection*)

The Thames completely frozen over, 14 January 1891, at the Hollows just west of Kew Bridge, on the north bank. (*Hounslow Cultural & Community Services, Local Studies Collection, Chiswick Library*)

The triumphal arch erected to celebrate the cessation of tolls on Kew Bridge, 8 February 1873. The cessation of tolls was a direct result of the purchase of the bridge by the Metropolitan Board of Works for £57,300. (*Hounslow Cultural &Community Services, Local Studies Collection, Chiswick Library*)

Kew Bridge and the waterworks at low tide, with the tower of Kew waterworks in the distance, *c.* 1900. The tower and surrounding buildings of Kew Steam Museum house five Cornish beam engines, including the world's largest surviving working engine, Grand Junction 90. (*Hounslow Cultural & Community Services, Local Studies Collection, Chiswick Library*)

The informal market near the fountain, Kew Bridge, *c.* 1892. Market gardeners would gather here to sell their goods and water their horses. In May 1893 the official Brentford Market opened. (*Hounslow Cultural & Community Services, Local Studies Collection, Chiswick Library*)

The Swan Uppers rounding up birds at Kew, 1930s. Swans were once a symbol of wealth power. More importantly, they were food. This ancient and colourful ceremony dates back at least to the fifteenth century and is still carried out each July to determine ownership of the new crop of cygnets. There are only three legal owners of swans on the Thames: the Crown and two livery companies, Dyers and Vintners. Once the swans and cygnets are spotted, a cry of 'all up' is heard and then the swans are rounded up for marking. Vintners' cygnets get a nick on each side of the beak and those belonging to the Dyers get one nick on the right. The cygnets of unmarked parents remain unmarked as they belong to the Crown. (*Michael Turk*)

Osier cutters enjoying tea and toast by the fire on Chiswick Eyot, 1927. The osier or willow rods were once grown all over islands in the Thames and harvested for use in a wide variety of products from fencing to eel traps. Behind the men are bundles of osiers tied into 'bolts' and stacked to dry out. These 'bolts' may have already been graded according to one of four sizes: Luke, Threepenny, Middleborough and Great. (*Hounslow Cultural & Community Services, Local Studies Department, Chiswick Library*)

Old Putney Bridge, probably photographed after 1870 when a barge damaged the wooden bridge, requiring the replacement of the centre span with one made of iron. (*The Environment Agency and The River & Rowing Museum*)

Putney Bridge and aqueduct, 1878. The new Putney Bridge was built on the line of the Chelsea waterworks aqueduct in this photograph. Note what appears to be the toll-bar swing-gate on the right. (*Mary Clarke*)

The commencement of construction of the new Putney Bridge with the old bridge in the background. Work started in 1882 and the Prince of Wales opened the new bridge on 29 May 1886. (*Wandsworth Borough Council*)

The Palace of Westminster, otherwise known as the Houses of Parliament, and the clock tower photographed from the river in the 1950s. The original palace was destroyed by fire in 1834 with only Westminster Hall, the jewel tower, the crypt of St Stephen's Chapel and some cloisters remaining. The clock tower is best known as 'Big Ben', the name that belongs to the bell inside, and is the largest public clock in the world. (*John Joslin*)

The *Prince of Wales* steamer departing from Victoria embankment, photographed by Henry Taunt in about 1900. In the background are Hungerford Railway Bridge and Charing Cross station. (*The Environment Agency*)

The shot tower at Waterloo Bridge, 1880. Built in 1886, this tower was used, as its name suggests, for the manufacture of lead shot. Molten lead with certain additives was dropped from the top of the tower through a sieve and from there it fell into a vat of cold water, forming reasonably spherical lead shot. To vary the size of the shot, different sieves were used. Bristol plumber William Watts patented this process in 1782 after supposedly dreaming about it. Despite its use in the 1951 Festival of Britain and having Grade II listed status, the shot tower was demolished in 1962. (*Oxfordshire County Council Photographic Archive*)

In the 1920s Waterloo Bridge suffered subsidence and this temporary iron structure was erected alongside while repairs were carried out. These proved to be short-lived and the bridge was replaced with the one we see today, which finally opened in 1942. (*Mary Clarke*)

The River Thames Police steam launch *Chowkidar* moored at Waterloo pier, *c.* 1900. Purchased from Germany in 1891, the vessel's unusual name is derived from the Hindustani for night watch. Possibly as a result of Sinn Fein's activities, Parliament felt vulnerable to attack from the river and this powered boat was introduced to patrol the area. Waterloo pier was bought second hand in 1872 to replace the original floating police station, *The Royalist*. One end of the pier had living quarters, bathroom, lounge, canteen and a library. The business end of the pier housed the police station with two cells, an office, recovery room, stores and a cycle rack. Because of the high number of suicides from Waterloo Bridge, the pier also had a specially designed 'jumpers' boat', which had a roller across the stern to assist with recoveries. It was said that if jumpers changed their minds on the way down, there would always be a rescue boat on hand to save them! (*The Thames Police Association Museum*)

'C' class submarines visiting Temple pier and probably photographed in the third week of July 1909, shortly after *C11* was sunk in a collision with the SS *Eddystone* near Cromer, Norfolk. Along with the depot ship HMS *Hazard* and the torpedo boat destroyer *Moy* were submarines *C12*, *C14*, *C15* and *C16*. 'C' class submarines were just over 130 ft long and 13 ft wide and had little in the way of comforts – no bulkheads, cabins, bunks, toilets, very little fresh water, and only a hot plate to cook on. The crew slept on the deck and had to carry out all of their tasks either sitting or stooped. (*The Environment Agency*)

The former shot tower on the South Bank was used at the Festival of Britain to beam messages to the moon. The 1951 Festival was intended to lift the country after the miseries of the Second World War, and included arts, science, technology and industrial design exhibitions. The incoming Conservative government swiftly cleared the site, fearing that it may have been considered a monument to socialism. Only the Royal Festival Hall was left as a reminder. (*John Joslin*)

There have been numerous bridges on this site since the first timber structure was thrown across by the Romans *c*. AD 43. Many of the subsequent timber bridges collapsed, perhaps sparking the nursery rhyme 'London Bridge is falling down'. The London Bridge that lasted for over 600 years was replaced in about 1825 by the bridge seen in this view. (*John Joslin*)

Steamers waiting at London Bridge, *c*. 1900. When London Bridge was sold to the United States in kit form, many thought that the 'gullible' Americans had been duped into thinking that they had bought Tower Bridge. London Bridge now resides in the very successful Lake Havasu holiday resort in Arizona. An interesting footnote: when the bridge was imported into the United States, it entered the country as a large antique! (*The Environment Agency and The River & Rowing Museum*)

Flying through Tower Bridge, 1912. This incident made aviation history because the pilot, Mr Maclean, continued on to fly under London and Cannon Street rail bridges, over the top of Southwark and the two Blackfriars Bridges, then under Waterloo, Charing Cross rail and Westminster bridges, hitting the water twice *en route*. Causing chaos at most of these bridges, he landed near the Houses of Parliament and later visited Bow Street magistrates court for his trouble. He was charged with endangering life by dangerously flying beneath the bridges. This crazy stunt has not been surpassed to this day. (*John Joslin*)

The East End on fire, September 1940. Enemy air raids were originally not intended for the capital but lost German planes dropped their bombs on London one night, sparking tit-for-tat raids. With the Thames providing a simple signpost, the numerous docks and warehouses in the East End took a battering. Fires of every description raged in the international goods stored there, the heat so intense that stinging particles of pepper filled the air and rivers of molten sugar ran down the streets. (*The Thames Police Association Museum*)

After the Second World War BOAC introduced flights using this Short Sunderland flying boat. Converted into a luxury airliner, the ex-Fleet Air Arm anti-submarine patrol aircraft is seen underneath the upraised arms of Tower Bridge before moving downstream to moor near the Tower for servicing. (*John Joslin*)

Sir Winston Churchill's coffin on board the Port of London Authority's launch *Havengore*, making its way up to Festival Pier on 30 January 1965. To the right, the dockers of Hays wharf gave a spontaneous tribute by dipping the jibs of their cranes. Overhead, four Lightnings swooped down to 500 ft in a noisy flypast, twelve more were to follow from RAF Squadrons 56 and 111, Wattisham and 19 and 92, Leconfield. Tough Brothers built the *Havengore* in 1956. In boat-building tradition, the men who constructed her stamped six pennies and bonded them into the keel. Found rotting near Gravesend, she was recently bought by New Zealand millionaire Owen Palmer for £75,000 and he has overseen her restoration. (*The Thames Police Association Museum*)

Hay barges, otherwise known as 'Stackies' for obvious reasons, outside the Tower of London, *c.* 1900. Entire books have been written about this famous building; suffice it to say that it has been many things in its 1,000-year history from menagerie to torture chamber. It is best known, however, for housing the Crown Jewels. (*Andy McGrandle*)

A Thames Police officer holds out his arm to rescue a man from the river. It is not clear where this man had found himself in difficulties; perhaps he was one of the jumpers mentioned earlier. Pulling someone on board a boat can be potentially dangerous for both parties; the person in the river can easily pull the rescuer in while they struggle to get on board. (*John Joslin*)

An aerial view of part of Surrey Commercial Docks. These docks were once a hotchpotch constructed by different developers. They were eventually amalgamated to be run by one company. The principal dock, Greenland, was best known for its association with whaling, but most of the other basins were given over to timber, some of which can be seen here. These docks were the domain of the stevedore (*estibador* is the Spanish word for packer) and the deal porters who carried seemingly impossible loads of wood across their shoulders. Albion dock, two-thirds of Canada, Island, Lady, Lavender, Norway, Quebec, Russia and Stave, along with 4 miles of the Surrey canal, have all gone. However, the names of some live on in roads and woodland. (*John Joslin*)

The Thames has frozen over several times. Here we see the reach near Limehouse in 1891. Freezing occurred so frequently during the eighteenth and nineteenth centuries that frost fairs were held on the river. These fairs had bear baiting, a bullring, various stalls, a fun fair and the roasting of an ox on the ice. There was even a semi-permanent shopping street set up, nicknamed City Road. (*The Thames Police Association Museum*)

Thames Police officers outside their Wapping headquarters, 1900. London's docks were once the envy of the world, but with the vast amount of incoming goods, thieving was rife. A local magistrate, Patrick Colquhoun wrote a treatise on policing the metropolis and among his ideas was the setting up of enclosed docks where the handling of cargoes could be scrutinized. The West India Company, who also paid for watchmen on the quays took on this idea and so, in this roundabout fashion, the oldest and the first police force in the world was formed on 2 July 1798. (*The Thames Police Association Museum*)

On 28 July 1947, after a long spell of hot weather, these boys spent their time diving into the Thames from Tower pier. (*The Thames Police Association Museum*)

The Canoe Camping Club's annual tideway-run taking a break on the foreshore outside the Prospect of Whitby pub in the late 1950s. Built in 1520, when it was known as the Devil's Tavern, the pub was later renamed after a collier from Whitby. The canoe run from Putney to Wapping and return would take about two and a half hours each way on the outgoing and incoming tides. Lunch was a hearty meal in one of the nearby dockers' cafés. (*Roger French*)

The tragic consequences of swimming in the river became all too apparent with the death of this unidentified lad who is attended to by the Thames Police. (*Associated Newspapers/Atlantic Syndication*)

The Union Dry Dock near the former Limehouse entrance to West India Docks was formed by the unusual method of sinking the East Indiaman vessel *Canton* in 1829. The decks and beams were removed along with the stern, which was replaced with lock gates, forming a small dry dock. The *Cutty Sark* was among the vessels overhauled in this unique dock, which was eventually demolished in 1898 and replaced with a more conventional structure. (© *National Maritime Museum, London*)

Concrete barges under construction in West India Docks, early 1940s. Made from pre-cast concrete slabs slotted together with concrete stiffening ribs cast in place to tie the whole structure together, these barges underwent rigorous sea-worthiness and water-tightness tests, which they passed with flying colours. Wates Construction, which made the vessels, was also involved in the building of the famous Mulberry floating harbours used to great effect off the coast of Normandy during the Second World War. (*Wates Construction*)

A 'Mammoth' crane manoeuvres a Wates cargo barge into position for launching at West India Docks, November 1944. By the previous month, Wates had built and launched 100 of these barges. They were launched sideways from the edge of the quay with a drop of just under 6 ft. Weighing in at 120 tons, their launch was said to be 'spectacular'. (*Wates Construction*)

The River Thames police boat *Watch* on patrol near New Dundee Wharf, *c.* 1900. In the dark on 3 September 1878 the worst disaster in British inland waters occurred when *The Bywell Castle* crashed amidships into the pleasure steamer *Princess Alice*, cutting it in two. She sank in four minutes with the loss of 640 lives. At the subsequent inquiry, it was asked why not one soul had been saved by the police in their rowing galleys. Probably stung by this criticism, the police pressed launches such as *The Watch* into service soon after. (*The Thames Police Association Museum*)

Fletcher's Wharf, Gravesend, 1890. Moored at the wharf is the topsail schooner *Martha*, built in 1880 by J.W. Tonkin of Cardiff and owned by W.J. Lodge, and the stumpy swim-head barge *Elizabeth*. On the right is the ancient pub called the Hit or Miss. Its age is not known, but it is said that the pub was once the haunt of smugglers and river pirates who used to meet in its cellars. In the background are the minarets of Clifton Marine baths, where hot and cold sea bathing was popular, as were the 'medicinal qualities' of the Thames mud. (© *National Maritime Museum, London*)

A rare photograph of one of the steamers operating on the Gravesend–Tilbury ferry. As steam-operated ferryboats only commenced working in 1883 with the introduction of the *Tilbury*, this could be either the *Earl of Leicester* or *Queen Elizabeth*, although a definite identification cannot be made. (*Gravesend Central Library*)

A distant view of Tilbury docks in about 1900 with the masts of ships just visible. The Tilbury Hotel was a popular landmark here until 1944 when it was bombed and burnt out completely. On the nearby marshes, with the Spanish fleet threatening to invade, Queen Elizabeth I made her famous rallying speech to her troops in August 1588; 'I know I have the body of a weak and feeble woman, but I have the heart and stomach of a king, and a king of England too. . . .' (*Andy McGrandle*)

Grays Beach, seen here in 1925, was created in 1906 to provide a facility for pleasure along with the park and gardens. The sand for the beach was imported from another famous resort, Great Yarmouth in Norfolk. (*Thurrock Local History Museum*)

Looking at a map of the estuary, it is hard to imagine that there was ever a wharf here as the small town of Fobbing is some distance from the river. A report of 1560 mentions Fobbing as a place to land, but not much in the way of regular shipping. Yet in this view of Fobbing wharf, there was obviously sufficient water for barges to sail up the creek for their cargoes of salt, chalk, butter, cheeses, wood, bricks and coal. (*Thurrock Local History Museum*)

One of the 'secret forts' being towed out into the estuary in the early 1940s for scuttling into position. Created by Guy Maunsell to defend the estuary from enemy attacks, this is the navy design. Of the four navy forts built, two remain in their original positions on sandbanks at Sunk Head and Knock John. The army-design forts were larger and saw further action in the 1960s as homes for pirate radio stations such as Radio Caroline and Radio Sutch. (*Imperial War Museum*)

ACKNOWLEDGEMENTS

This volume would not have been possible without the generous help of the individuals and organisations listed below. I am very pleased to acknowledge everyone's help, time and interest and apologies to anyone I may have omitted. While every effort has been made to trace the owners or copyright holders of these photographs, it is possible some errors may have occurred. If this is the case, corrections will be made in later editions. During the compilation of this volume, I have consulted many reference sources including internet sites too numerous to include in a bibliography.

Alex Abbey-Taylor, Martin Adams, Valerie Andrews-Jones, Bob Aspinall, Nick Baker, Rebecca Barnard, Joanna Barrett, Frank Bayley, John Bayley, Mark Bayley, Jane Baxter, David Beasley, Alan Beaven, Ted Bell, Caroline Benson, David Birch, Peter Bird, Mark Blackwell, Michael Bott, Dr Rachel Brown, Catherine Britton, Mary Burge, Ashley Cairns, Jock Cairns, Margaret Calcott-James, Steve Capel-Davis, Terry Carney, Jonathon Catton, Betty Chaplin, Barbara Chilton, Rosemary Christian, Mary Clarke, Peter Clarke, Angela Collett, John Cook, Debbie Corner, Christopher Cove-Smith, Bob Cross, Pat Curtis, Dorothy Davis, Meredith Davis, Ron Davis, Nigel Dawe, Christopher Dodd, Matthew Duncan, John Emmett, John Evans, Tim Everson, G. Faulkner, Leigh Fenton, Dr Robert Fielden, Hilary Fisher, Dr Christopher French, Roger French, Paul Frost, Julia Gibbs, Frank Godsell, Gillian Goodbright, Olivia Gooden, Darran Gough, Dr Malcolm Graham, Joe Green, Wendy Griffin, Chris Groves, Alicia Gurney, Ian Halls, Carolyn Hammond, Georgie Hammond, Bill Harding, Roger Harding, Barbara Harris, Colin Harris, Vickie Harris, Beryl Hedges, David Hemingway, Ken Howe, Dr Judith Hunter, Julian Hunt, Roy Jamieson, Bob Jeffries, John Joslin, Vic Kettle, Mary Kool, David Lawrence, Emily Leach, Keith Lintott, Frank Lockhart, Iain MacKenzie, Ken Major, Pamela Marson, Paul Mason, Bill McCreadie, Andy McGrandle, John McNeil, John Mills, L.C. Morrison, Mark Murray-Flutter, David Messum, Roger Mutton, Doris Neville-Davies, Steve Newman, Stephen Nicholls, Alison Norcross, Dave Norris, Jaap Oepkes, Dominique Oliver, Lorna Orton, David Packer, Martin Packer, Graham Parlour, Ralph Parsons, Dick Paterson, Graham Peek, Robert Pitcher, P.E. Platt, Nick Pollard, Sheila Potts, John Powell, Penny Radford, Rowland Raynor, John Redmond, Sandra Roe, Rachael Rogers, Michael Rowe, Peter Russell, Carah Salisbury, Meredith Sampson, D.Shaw, Gordon Shilleto, John Shore, M.Simms, Joey Sims, Paul Sims, D.H. Simpson, Eleanor Simpson, Margaret Simpson, Ken Smith, Wendy Songest, Carol Spicer, John Spittle, David Taylor, Vivienne Taylor, Vivienne Thomas, Norman Timms, Ken Townsend, Lucie Tucker, Victor Tucker, Michael Turk, Jean Tyler, Peter Tyler, Christine Vickers, Neil White, M. White, David Wilson.

Air History Branch (RAF), Amateur Rowing Association, Atlantic Syndication, Bensington Society, Birmingham Gun Barrel Proof House, The Bodleian Library (University of Oxford), Britannia Refined Metals, British Canoe Union, British Waterways, Brick Information Service, Centre for Oxfordshire Studies, Chertsey Museum, Chiswick Library, Colourbox Techunique, Egham-by-Runnymede Historical Society, Egham Museum Trust, Elmbridge Museum, Environment Agency, Eton College, Goring and Streatley Local History Society, Gravesend Central Library, History of Reading Society, Imperial War Museum, Inland Waterways Association, Marlow Society, Maidenhead Library, Ministry of Defence, National Rivers Authority, National Maritime Museum, National Waterways Museum, The Putney Society, Richmond Library, Richmond Local History Society, Reading Civic Society, River & Rowing Museum, River Thames Society, Royal Armouries, Royal Navy Admiralty Library, Royal Navy Submarine Museum, Rural History Centre (University of Reading), Spelthorne Museum, Sunbury and Shepperton Local History Society, Thames Police Association Museum, Thames Water, Thurrock Museum, TWR Group, Walton Library, Wandsworth Borough Council, Warborough and Shillingford Local History Society, Wates Construction, Windsor Collection, Worshipful Company of Gunmakers.

A special mention for Louise Mullaney's constructive comments, David Rogers' computer expertise and Simon Fletcher's faith in my original idea that became 'Along the Thames'.

BRITAIN IN OLD PHOTOGRAPHS

Northamptonshire

Northampton Past &
  Present

Nottinghamshire

Arnold & Bestwood:
  A Second Selection
Kirkby in Ashfield:
  A Second Selection
Nottinghamshire at Work
Nottingham Past & Present

Oxfordshire

Around Abingdon
Around Didcot
Around Henley-on-Thames
Around Wheatley
Around Witney
Around Woodstock
Banbury
Banbury Past & Present
Cowley & East Oxford Past
  & Present
Forgotten Thames
Garsington
Henley-on-Thames Past &
  Present
Literary Oxford
Oxford
Oxfordshire at Play
Oxfordshire at School
Wantage, Faringdon & The
  Vale Villages
Witney

Shropshire

Shropshire Railways
South Shropshire
Telford

Somerset

Chard & Ilminster

Staffordshire

Aldridge Revisited
Kinver & Enville: A Second
  Selection

Newcastle-under-Lyme Past
  & Present
Pattingham & Wombourne
Stafford
Stoke-on-Trent Past &
  Present

Suffolk

Bury St Edmunds
Lowestoft Past & Present
Southwold
Stowmarket
Suffolk Transport
Suffolk at Work: A Second
  Selection

Surrey

Cheam & Belmont
Esher
Richmond
Walton upon Thames &
  Weybridge

Sussex

Around East Grinstead
Around Heathfield:
  A Second Selection
Bishopstone & Seaford:
  A Second Selection
Eastbourne Past & Present
High Weald: A Second
  Selection
Horsham Past & Present
Lancing
Palace Pier, Brighton
RAF Tangmere
Rye & Winchelsea

Tyne & Wear

Whitley Bay

Warwickshire

Around Leamington Spa
Around Leamington Spa:
  A Second Selection
Around Bulkington
Bedworth Past & Present
Knowle & Dorridge

Nuneaton Past & Present
Rugby: A Second Selection
Warwickshire Railways

West Midlands

Bilston, Bradley &
  Ladymoor
Birmingham Transport
Black Country Pubs
Blackheath
Cradley Heath
Cradley Heath: A Second
  Selection
Darlaston, Moxley &
  Bentley
Great Bridge & District
Halesowen: A Second
  Selection
Ladywood
Ladywood Revisited
Lye & Wollescote
Lye & Wollescote: A Second
  Selection
Northfield Past & Present
Oldbury
Rowley
Sedgley: A Fourth Selection
Smethwick
Solihull
Stourbridge, Wollaston &
  Amblecote
Stourbridge, Wollaston &
  Amblecote: A Second
  Selection
Tipton: A Third Selection
Wednesbury
Wordsley

Wiltshire

Around Devizes
Around Highworth
Castle Combe to
  Malmesbury
Crewkerne & the Ham
  Stone Villages
Marlborough: A Second
  Selection
Salisbury: A Second
  Selection

Worcestershire

Worcester Past & Present

Yorkshire

Around Hoyland
Around Hoyland: A Second
  Selection
Doncaster
Huddersfield
Huddersfield: A Second
  Selection
Leeds in the News
Northallerton: A Second
  Selection
Pontefract
Sheffield
Shire Green, Wincobank &
  Ecclesfield
Wombwell & Darfield

Wales

Anglesey
Carmarthen & the Tywi
  Valley
Chepstow & The River
  Wye
Haverfordwest
Milford Haven
Upper Teifi
Welshpool

Scotland

Annandale
Around Lochaber
Clydesdale
Musselburgh
Perth
Selkirkshire
St Andrews

Ireland

Coleraine & the Causeway
  Coast

To order any of these titles please telephone our distributor,
Haynes Publishing, on 01963 442105
For a catalogue of these and our other titles please telephone
Joanne Govier at Sutton Publishing on 01453 732423